DAILY LIFE

AND

WORK IN INDIA

DAILY LIFE

AND

WORK IN INDIA

W. J. WILKINS

WITH FIFTY-NINE ILLUSTRATIONS

GYAN

Published by

Gyan Publishing House
5, Ansari Road
Daryaganj, New Delhi-110002
Phone: 011-47034999, 9811692060
E-mail: books@gyanbooks.com

Distribution Network
gyanbooks.com
India, USA, Canada, UK, Australia, France

ISBN: 978-81-212-9332-7 (PB)
First Published, 1888

2nd Impression 2023

Printed at: Gyan Press, Delhi.

DAILY LIFE AND WORK IN INDIA

Author: W. J. WILKINS

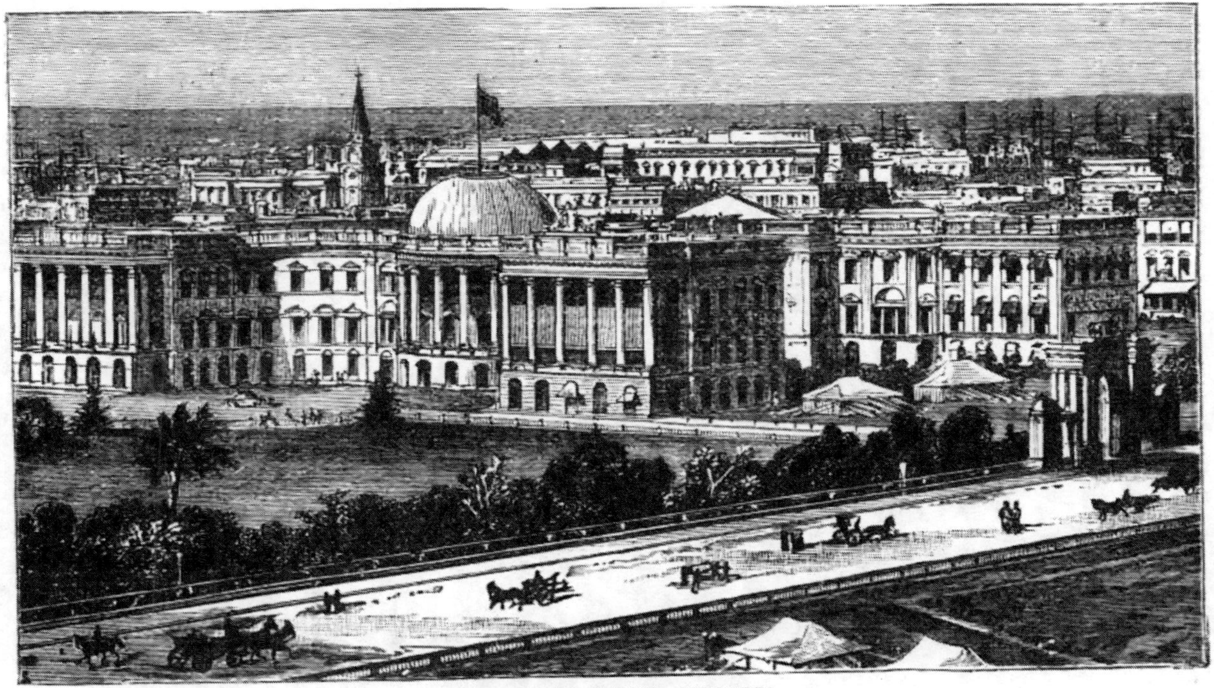

GOVERNMENT HOUSE, CALCUTTA.

DAILY LIFE

AND

WORK IN INDIA

BY

W. J. WILKINS

AUTHOR OF "HINDU MYTHOLOGY," "MODERN HINDUISM," ETC., ETC.

LONDON MISSIONARY SOCIETY'S EDITION

WITH FIFTY-NINE ILLUSTRATIONS

London

T. FISHER UNWIN

26 PATERNOSTER SQUARE

MDCCCLXXXVIII

To

MY

CHILDREN.

PREFACE.

THIS book owes its origin to the suggestion of some good friends of Missions who thought that a work describing the ordinary life of people in India, and the different forms of Mission work as it is carried on amongst them, could not fail to interest both young and old. In carrying out this suggestion, I have given a series of sketches of the city of Calcutta and the district, with its European and native population. I have described the homes, schools, manners and customs of the people, their religious faiths and practices; and spoken too of some of their temples and other holy places. I have also attempted to show how the missionaries work and travel as they seek to unfold before the myriads of Hindus the "unsearchable riches of Christ."

The writing of this work has given me intense pleasure, as it has compelled me to live over again some of the happiest years of my life, and brought back to view scenes and people that had almost faded from memory. I can only wish that my readers may have as great delight in forming the acquaintance of some of these, as I have had in recalling them to mind. If, in addition to this, it awakens their sympathies on behalf of India's millions who "sit in darkness and in the region and shadow of death," and leads them to pray and work for their enlightenment, I shall be truly thankful that it was undertaken.

W. J. WILKINS.

Leeds.

LIST OF ILLUSTRATIONS.

CONTENTS.

CHAPTER IV.

THE PEOPLE GENERALLY.

CHAPTER V.

A TALK ABOUT INSECTS, REPTILES, &c.

CHAPTER VI.

A CHAPTER ABOUT THE GODS.

CHAPTER VII.

HINDU TEMPLES.

CHAPTER VIII.

HOLY PLACES AND PILGRIMS.

CHAPTER IX.

RELIGIOUS FESTIVALS.

CHAPTER X.

GURUS, OR RELIGIOUS TEACHERS, AND THEIR DISCIPLES.

CHAPTER XI.

HINDU SAINTS.

CHAPTER XII.

BURNING GHÀTS AND TREATMENT OF THE DYING.

CHAPTER XIII.

BAZAAR PREACHING.

CHAPTER XIV.

LIFE ON THE RIVERS.

CHAPTER XV.

LIFE IN TENT.

PAGE

CHAPTER XVI.

ALL ABOUT TIGERS.

CHAPTER XVII.

SCHOOL WORK.

CHAPTER XVIII.

WORK AMONGST THE HINDU GIRLS AND WOMEN.

CHAPTER XIX.

INDIA'S NEED.

DAILY LIFE AND WORK IN INDIA.

CHAPTER I.

CALCUTTA.

BEFORE describing the people of Calcutta, it is necessary that a little should be said about the city in which they live, in order that some idea may be formed of their surroundings.

English people who have not travelled seem to have an idea that all countries must be like England, or, if unlike, necessarily inferior. But a stranger arriving in Calcutta is agreeably surprised to find himself in streets in many respects far prettier than those of most English towns; the trees on either side of the road, with their bright green leaves and gorgeous flowers, giving an appearance of country life even in the midst of a populous city.

The city of Calcutta stretches for a space of about seven miles along the bank of the river Hugli, a branch of the great river Ganges. Originally the stream flowed through another channel some two miles away, but, quite in harmony with the custom of rivers in India, it decided to change its course, and left the great temple at Kāli Ghāt, which had been built on its banks, by the side of a narrow stream—the original bed of the Ganges. So convinced are the Hindus of this fact, that for a considerable length of the river Hugli no Hindus are burned on its banks, because it is supposed to have lost its charm there; but above the part where this little stream leaves the larger one, and after it has again fallen into it, the dead are burned, in the certain hope of obtaining happy entrance into heaven by this act. The city, though long, is not much more than a mile wide, yet in this space about 700,000 people reside; or if those of the suburbs be added, they number over 1,000,000. The streets are mostly in the direction of the river, with others intersecting them at right angles; but there are some tortuous narrow lanes that would equal those of almost any English town. The city is perfectly flat, the only even slightly rising ground being the approaches to bridges over the narrow stream above mentioned.

The river Hugli, by which Calcutta is reached, is most difficult for navigators. There are immense sand-banks, which, constantly shifting, render it necessary to keep men always employed in taking soundings, who send up reports of the position of these banks to the city several times a day for the guidance of the pilots. A safe channel to-day may be dangerous to-morrow. I shall not forget the sense of danger that was produced when sailing up the river for the first time. At two places men stood hatchet in hand to cut the hawser by which our vessel was being towed, so that, in case we touched the ground, the steamer might not be dragged down with the ship. I have heard of ships colliding near these sand-banks being completely out of sight within five minutes.

On sailing up the river, the first sight that interests one in nearing the city is the residence of the late

A EUROPEAN RESIDENCE IN CALCUTTA.

ruler of Oudh. When the British Government took possession of his territory he was brought to Calcutta, and a large tract of land, together with a handsome pension, was granted to him. In these grounds a number of houses have been built for himself and his numerous household. As some of these are of various bright colours—blue, green, red, &c.—they look rather gaudy. Inside the grounds are beautiful tanks with marble steps, and the finest collection of water birds and snakes in India. He also keeps thousands of pigeons, and it is a most interesting sight to watch them flying about in large flocks. This is said to be one of the chief amusements of the king. The old man frequently goes out for a drive in an old-fashioned chariot, attended by about twenty troopers. The men are very dirty, badly dressed, badly mounted, are poor riders, and most unsoldierly in appearance. The attendants of a third-rate circus in a procession through an English village are quite respectable compared with this royal body-guard.

After sailing for a little longer, the next object of importance that comes in sight is Fort William, a large and strong defence. It was a most grateful sight, after sixteen weeks at sea, to catch sight of the Union Jack floating nobly from this fort, and to know that, though far away from England, we were still to live under British rule.

To give a clear idea of a city to those who have not seen it, is not easy. Still, I wish to try to enable those who have not visited Calcutta to have some idea of what it is like.

The city may be roughly divided into two parts—

the European and the Native; though in the native part some Europeans live, and in the European part some natives are to be found. The European part of the city covers about a square mile. Here are to be found the fine houses that have given to Calcutta the name of "The City of Palaces." These buildings are all detached, each standing in its own grounds. They are built of brick, and plastered; so that every few years it is necessary for the plaster to be repaired, and a new coat of colour given to the whole.

FLAT ROOF OF HOUSE, WITH TOP OF STAIRCASE.

Owing to the saltpetre in the clay with which the bricks are made, the houses generally look rather scabby, especially near the ground; but when the walls are newly finished and the Venetians have received a fresh coat of green paint, a Calcutta house looks very pretty. Of all the places I have seen since my return to Europe, Jersey reminds me most of India.

These houses vary little in style. As was the custom in England a generation back, houses are built very much like each other. The style is mostly Doric; and when the building is three stories high, with a broad verandah on two or three sides, each supported by massive pillars, there is something palatial in their appearance. For an illumination, I know no city that is better fitted for an effective display. All the houses have flat roofs, on which it is most pleasant to sit or walk in the early morning or after the sun has set. Formerly the grounds of each house were surrounded by a high wall; but the fashion—and a good one it is—has set in in favour of cast-iron railings instead. As the gardens are tastefully laid out, these, together with the clean white walls of the house and the green Venetians, form a very attractive picture. Many of our manufacturing towns in England certainly look ugly and uninteresting to one who has spent many years in a place like Calcutta.

The plan of these houses is a very simple one; there is not much architectural ingenuity or variety displayed in them. The typical Calcutta house has a hall in the centre, with two rooms on either side, each having its bath-room; the hall on the ground-floor serving for dining-room, and that on the first floor for drawing-room. There are no underground rooms or cellars, as in the rainy season the water is only about three or four feet from the surface. When people cannot afford to rent a whole house—and rents in Calcutta are exceedingly high—they take a flat; so that in many large houses there are two or even three families living. I have known £100 a year to be paid for a couple of rooms on the third or uppermost flat of a house in the heart of the city.

Along the bank of the Hugli is the Strand—the drive or Rotten Row of Calcutta, at one end of which are the Eden Gardens, a most beautifully laid-out spot, where a military band discourses sweet music as the sun goes down. There, for about half an hour, all Calcutta assembles. Many leave their carriages for a promenade; whilst others remain seated and their friends come to chat with them there. It is most interesting to walk through the gardens at this hour, as there would hardly be found in any part of the world a more diversified crowd. It is a cosmopolitan gathering—Europe and Asia, Africa and America, are represented; whilst the ubiquitous Jew is also present in good numbers. I certainly have never seen in any place a more interesting gathering of the various branches of the human family than is to be met with evening after evening in these gardens. The whole place is brilliantly illuminated with gas and the electric light.

On one or two evenings in the week there is a slight diversion from the gardens by the river. Calcutta can boast of a Zoo, beautifully laid out, and well stocked with animals, birds, and reptiles. This was the result of the immense energy and artistic taste of Sir R. Temple. In about a couple of years, a dirty, ugly village and a piece of waste land were transformed into a beautiful garden with its lakes and hills, and houses for specimens of the animal world from distant countries as well as from all parts of India. It is a marvel of ingenuity and perseverance, and it would be difficult to name any place where one could spend a pleasanter hour than in the Zoo in Calcutta. The birds and animals usually found at such places in Europe, where they need to be carefully guarded against the cold, are at home in a climate such as that of India, and are as happy as caged animals can possibly be. As a band plays in the gardens on certain evenings, a good number of Calcutta people find their way there.

Between the European part of the city and the river, in front of the fort, is the Maidān, a plain about a mile and a quarter across. This forms the parade ground for the troops; an exercise ground for a goodly number of Europeans and natives who are wise enough to get up early in the morning for a ride, drive, or walk; a place where football, cricket, polo, and lawn tennis are played in the evening; and often, too, it is the camping ground for native or European troops for whom the fort cannot provide sufficient accommodation. Round this plain rise some of the best European residences, and the view across it to the river when the rains have refreshed the earth, the tall masts of the ships forming a background, is one not soon to be forgotton.

On the Strand road at drive-time may be seen almost every kind of vehicle from the four-in-hand coach to the little pony carriage. Barouches, broughams, landaus, phaetons, roll along; also the buggy, or hooded gig, the dog-cart, and mail-phaeton. The typical local conveyance is a palki gharry; *i.e.*, a square box on wheels. There are several modifications of this ugly conveyance; but though very comfortable and serviceable on sunny days or in the rainy season, they are not at all comfortable in the evening or morning, when the object of the drive is simply to get a little fresh air. Numbers of ladies and gentlemen ride; so the Strand presents quite a gay scene. Walking there, one does not feel that India is a land of barbarism.

AN INDIAN TRAVELLING CARRIAGE.

Whilst these grand equipages are driving along,

some earnest seekers after health try to keep their livers in order by a walk, whilst others are carried along in the palanquin, better known in Calcutta as the palki. This is certainly *one* of the most uncomfortable modes of conveyance—to lie in a semi-recumbent posture, having no comfortable resting-place for the head. The palki-bearers are quite an institution in the city. They stand at the corner of every street, and seem to regard it as a personal injury to themselves that a European should walk through the streets. As there are four men to each palki, and each is anxious for a fare, it is most difficult to get along without being irritated by the cry, "Palki, saheb! Palki, saheb!" These men with their conveyance are far more trying to one's patience than the news-boys in a London street. A story is told of a sailor who, wishing to see as much as possible of the city, could not be persuaded to ride inside a palki, but, mounting on the top, made the men carry him in this way—to them as sensible a procedure as it would be for a man to sit on the top of a cab rather than inside. To these vehicles must be added the jinriksha, or man-carriage of Japan, a sort of buggy drawn by a man; and also the English bicycle and tricycle.

A word or two about the churches. Although so far from Europe, there seems to be ample provision for various spiritual tastes. First comes the cathedral, a pretty but by no means imposing structure, for which India is indebted to Bishop Wilson. This is the most fashionable congregation in the city. A capital organ, a well-trained choir, and an ornate service render it most attractive. In addition to this

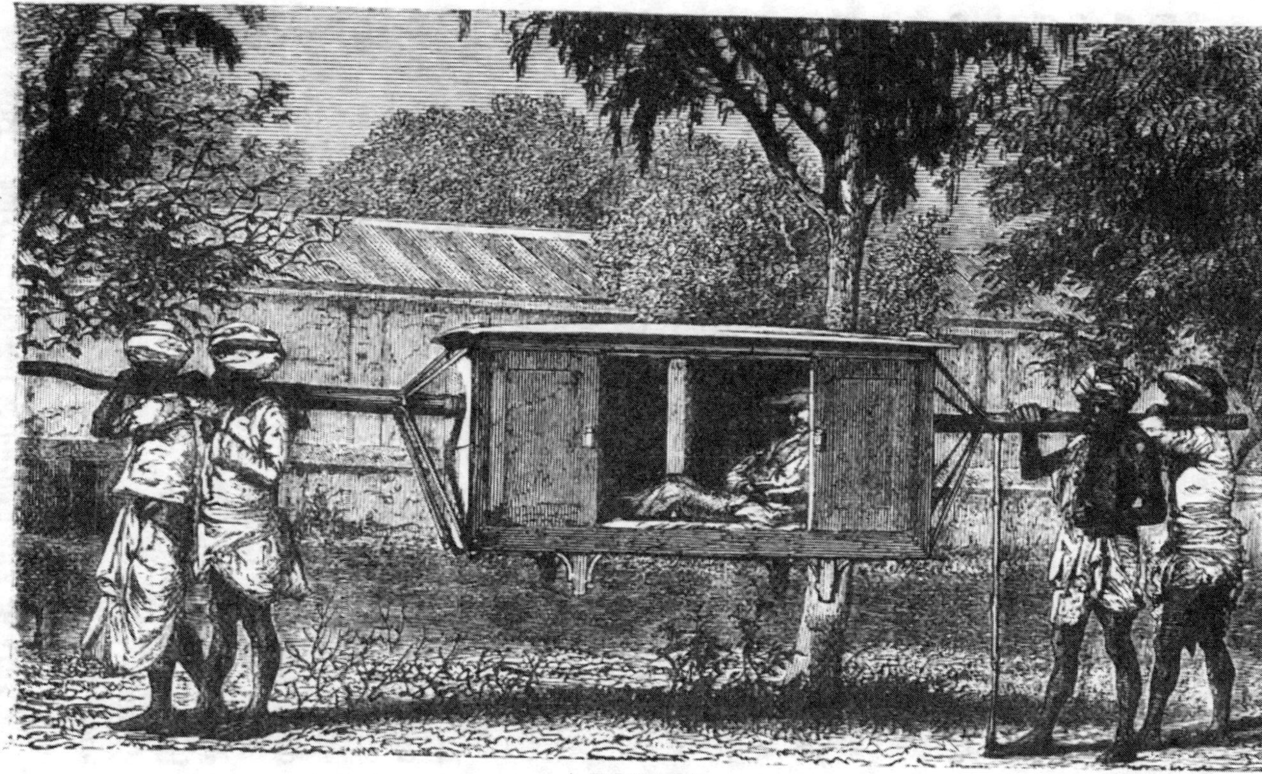

A PALANQUIN.

there are several Churches of England, to all of which, excepting one supplied by the missionaries of the Church Missionary Society, Government chaplains are appointed. Then there is one of the Established and one of the Free Church of Scotland; an Episcopal Methodist Church of America, and a Wesleyan Methodist; two Baptist and two Congregational churches. There are also three societies of Plymouth Brethren, one free, one very close, and one composed of two members only, who separated from the stricter party because they felt that their members ought not to preach the gospel to the heathen. Their position is this: if God wishes the heathen to be converted, He will accomplish this work without human aid. There are also six Roman Catholic churches. None of the churches are remarkable for their beauty or grandeur. In most of them arm-chairs take the place of pews; and for nine months in the year punkahs sway to and fro over the heads of the congregation to keep them cool in body, and so conduce to calmness of spirit during the service. The buildings of the Brahmos, or Hindus who have given up idol-worship and caste, should also be added to the places of worship, as in external appearance and internal arrangements they differ but little from them.

In walking about the city, one cannot fail to be struck with the number of tanks; where in an English town the centre of a square is adorned with a flower-garden or shrubbery, in Calcutta we have a sheet of water called a tank, often with plants growing round the edges. Formerly these tanks were necessary as water supplies for the district. But now there is a good water-works system, they remain to beautify, and possibly in some cases tend to preserve the health of the city. Some of the people, however, still prefer to take their water from the tanks rather than from the pipes. In the choice of water as in

INTERIOR OF CATHEDRAL, CALCUTTA, SHOWING THE PUNKAHS.

other matters, men differ in their ideas. I have seen many who prefer to drink the muddy and unfiltered water from a tank rather than the pure water from the pipe: they say the one is sweet, the other tasteless!

A word or two must be said about the river, with its splendid fleet of ships of all nations. At Calcutta it is fully a quarter of a mile wide, and is spanned by a pontoon bridge. Formerly, passengers were dependent upon a ferry steamer, or had to cross in some of the small boats, or dinghies as they are called; but the bridge being strong and wide, it is easy to drive across. As, however, the docks are above the bridge, and as some of the large ships occasionally anchor above it, twice a week this heavy structure is

A DINGHY.

opened, and a passage made by which they can go up or down. Craft of all kinds are to be seen. Sometimes there is a man-of-war in the harbour; the splendid fleets of the Peninsular and Oriental Co., the British India, and the City Line are always represented. There are also some of the largest sailing ships afloat, and some of the Chittagong ships—strong ships whose boards are *tied* together, without a single nail. There are passenger boats of every description, the dinghy being perhaps the one that is peculiar to North India. It is surprising in going from port to port to see the different shape and style of boat that is in use; and yet it would be hard to improve upon what we see. These dinghies are heavy, cumbersome-looking craft, but they seem to serve the purpose better than our own English boats would do.

As there is a large number of sailors always in port, formerly there was an immense amount of drunkenness amongst them. Those who have never made a long voyage cannot understand the position of a man when he is once more on *terra firma.* The lengthened imprisonment over for a time, the men are ready for any amusement that offers; and as until a few years ago the only places on shore for Jack were the grog-shops, it was no wonder that he found his way there, and became intoxicated. But this has now to a large extent passed away. A splendid Sailors' Home has been built, where concerts are given by the philanthropic friends of the sailor. On the floating Bethel of the Church of England Seamen's Mission a similar entertainment is provided. The Episcopal Methodists of America have opened two coffee-rooms in most convenient situations for the men. There religious services are provided, and reading-rooms with games and accommodation for writing; whilst for apprentices a tea meeting and service is held at the Y.M.C.A. rooms. I have heard many officers of ships declare that at no port in the world are the sailors better cared for than in Calcutta. And many are the stories told of young and old finding their way to God at the services held for them in this far-off city.

Passing from the English part of the town, we come to the Native. This is not an old city, but has grown into its present size since the English made it the capital of India. There were formerly a few villages, which have been largely replaced by densely populated streets. It is amusing and rather puzzling at first, when going about in the European quarter, to find that the new and high-sounding names of Victoria Square, &c., are not at all understood by the drivers and palki men; but that Nāpit Bazaar, *i.e.* the Barbers' bazaar, and Bāmun Busti, the Brāhmans' village, are still the names familiar to the people. These, once native villages or quarters of certain classes, have given place to the streets where the Europeans live; and in like manner, villages once distant now form parts of a continuous town. A few old houses are to be seen in the native quarter, but most of them are not much more than a hundred years old.

The first thing that strikes a stranger in walking through the streets of the native part of the town, is the way in which all a man's goods are exposed to view. There are no windows in which a few samples are exposed, whilst the stock is kept packed away on shelves; but in the purely native shops everything is visible at once. Those who were fortunate enough to see the Indian and Colonial Exhibition in London, had an opportunity of seeing a couple of shops exactly as they are seen in the Indian towns and villages. The shopkeeper sits or stands in front, selling his wares, often in very small quantities. So small are many of the transactions of the village shopkeepers, that shells (cowries) are used as money.

The smallest copper coin in circulation is the pice, the value of which is $\frac{1}{4}$ of $1\frac{1}{2}$d.; this is worth eighty cowries, and with these shells a good deal of business is transacted. In some towns of England farthings are not taken; how would the tradespeople like to have to do with shells of which about fifty go to the farthing?

The next thing one notices, is the way in which the people carry on their work in the open shops, where their goods are exposed for sale. If you want to purchase a stationery box, you go into a shop with its front wide open, and see the boxes in all stages of progress; or a picture of an idol, in like manner you see the artists at work with their brushes. Blacksmiths, carpenters, brass-workers, jewellers, &c., all work in sight of the world, and do not appear to be at all ashamed of being seen, or hindered by the passers-by. I have heard people speak of the Hindus as lazy; but certainly we see nothing of this as we walk through the streets. All appear to be hard at work. The purely native shops—*i.e.*, those where goods that are needed only by the natives can be obtained—are open, and work begins early in the morning, continuing until about eleven o'clock. They are then closed, and the work-people go away for their bath and morning meal. About two o'clock they re-open, and remain open until nine or ten at night. A walk through the streets is most interesting. Nothing is more surprising than to see the beautiful results in chasing in brass-work, or the carvings in ivory, and then to examine the clumsy tools with which this is done. The use that is made of the toes, too, is astonishing.

A carpenter's bench is never used; the carpenters squat to their work and use their toes to hold the wood they are planing;—certainly the Bengali work-

TINMEN TINNING COOKING VESSELS.

man is a four-handed man, whilst we, by the use of boots, have gone back to be two-handed.

In the native part of the city are to be found

the mansions of the best Hindu families. Many of these are very large, as they have to accommodate two hundred or more people. The Hindu idea of a family is very different from the English. When a man marries in England, he thinks it his duty to provide a house and establishment of his own, quite distinct from his father's and brothers'; but the Hindu boy-bridegroom takes his new wife to his father's house, where a bedroom is given to him. In some of these mansions there are four generations of people living together; not only the immediate descendants—*i.e.* the sons, grandsons, and great-grandsons of the karta or head of the family; but his brothers and their descendants too. Nor do they only live together; all the money the various members earn is put into a common fund, over the expenditure of which the karta rules.

In these large houses, which are generally built in the Classic style of architecture, having verandahs supported by massive Corinthian pillars, there are the outer and inner apartments quite distinct from each other; the outer being for the gentlemen and their visitors, the inner for the ladies. During the day, except at meal times, the gentlemen remain in their part of the house, as it is considered contrary to good etiquette for a man to be seen speaking to his wife by day. I have read of a bishop in the early Church being gravely censured for kissing his wife in the presence of his children; but Hindu custom goes beyond that—husband and wife must not speak to each other in the presence of the family. In the open courtyard of these houses the religious festivals are held.

The houses of the poor people are of a very different style. These are built of mud or matting, with tiled or thatched roofs, and have no glass windows — simply a little lattice-work to admit light and air, many of them being even destitute of this, and are quite dark when the doors are closed. They, too, have their verandah, and a family—according to our notions of a family, consisting of husband, wife and children—occupies a separate house.

The place of interest to all new-comers in Calcutta,

A BENGALI HUT.

is China Bazaar. This is a narrow street in which shops of all kinds have been opened by natives, almost exclusively for the supply of goods to Europeans. Bengalis and other natives, of course, are to be found amongst the customers; but it is mostly Europeans that frequent it. These shops are supplied with all kinds of European goods, and also the productions of distant parts of India, China, &c. Walking along about ten a.m., you notice each shop is carefully locked with two, three, or even four large padlocks. In a little time, a respectably dressed Bengali comes to the shop, but he has the key of *one* lock only; he must wait until his partners' arrival; and when all are present, the locks are removed and the door opened. This mutual distrust is very common amongst the people. When the shops are opened, the business of the day commences, and a lively scene it is. A stranger is pestered as he walks along the street, or his carriage is stopped without his orders by the touts, who declare that you are certain to get whatever you may require at *his* shop; and further, that at his shop you will have honest men to deal with, whilst at all his rivals there are only liars and rogues. At times, the dispute between the rival touts gets loud and angry in *words;* you need never fear anything beyond this, though the foulest abuse will be launched on the female relatives of the quarrellers. In these shops, ladies find tailors (men) at work trimming hats and bonnets, with a fashion-plate of the *Queen,* or *Myra's Journal* before them; men also making jackets, dresses, &c., from similar designs. The touts declare, "In my shop you everything get;" and though this is a somewhat exaggerated statement, it is true that either at his shop or his neighbours' in China Bazaar you will meet with almost everything that you can require, and often at prices but little above those asked in small English towns. Formerly, these dealers were supplied by the English merchants; now the manufacturers of England send their travellers to India, and their goods are sent direct to the native shopkeepers. When one is not in a hurry, there is often an immense amount of fun to be had in a walk through China Bazaar; but if in a hurry, it is most exasperating, because of the time wasted in chaffering over a purchase. If an article is honestly worth a shilling, about half a crown or three shillings is asked. The purchaser offers sixpence, and gradually the two approach until the proper price is reached. After a lengthened residence in India, when a man is known to the dealers, a word is enough sometimes to bring them down to the proper price. The excuse made for this mode of transacting business, is the fact that if they asked a fair price at first customers would want something taken off; so they put on an enormous price, in the expectation that they will have to come down. I believe that the dealers are better pleased (perhaps this is true of both buyer and seller) when by hard talking, sometimes it is hard lying, they have made a better bargain than they had expected.

I should say that though we have no omnibuses running through the streets, there are the palkis, and innumerable hired carriages, generally of the box type; but of late years we have had tram-cars in the heart of the city drawn by horses, and in the suburbs by steam-engines, which Leeds has supplied. At first there was a little prejudice against the trams, but now they are found to be so very convenient that all classes gladly avail themselves of them.

A description of Calcutta would hardly be complete without some notice of the Botanical Gardens, which lie a little below the city on the opposite side of the river. These gardens are managed by the Government, and are beautifully kept. The orchid, croton, and palm houses are most beautiful. Where in England we have glass houses with a heating apparatus in which tropical plants are reared, in the Calcutta gardens we have *cool* houses; the object being to obtain light without the bright sunbeams. These houses have an iron framework, with sides and roof of wire netting. On this, thin layers of grass are spread, by which means the plants are protected from the intense heat though they have a sufficiency of light. The crotons at Kew Gardens look poor compared with those in Calcutta. *The*

A BANYAN TREE, CALCUTTA.

attraction of the gardens, however, are the two banyan trees, one of which is said to be large enough to shade ten thousand men. The new branches of this tree run down hollow bamboos until they touch the ground, where they take root, and become supporters and feeders of the older parts of the tree. There seems to be no reason why, in time, one of these trees should not grow until its branches spread for miles. In the cold season, picnic parties are common in Calcutta; and to those who have often had their arrangements upset by the rain in

England, it comes as a pleasant surprise that they can make their arrangements for a party weeks or months beforehand with the certainty of having suitable weather.

There is one drawback to life even in this city, viz., the fearful cyclones that occasionally sweep across it. In 1864 there was a terrible storm, and as before its force was spent the wind blew directly up the river, it caused a wave about twenty feet high to rise, which tore away most of the ships from their moorings, and lifted several some distance inland. The waters swept over Saugar Island near the mouth of the river, and it was estimated that about twenty thousand people were drowned by it. In 1867 a second came, the force of which I felt. The strong walls of the house in which I was living swayed to and fro, the doors and windows of one side being carried away. I saw a piece of corrugated iron that was carried from the theatre with such force, that as it struck against the corner of a building near it was bent like a sheet of paper. Fortunately these do not visit the city very frequently; or rather, the centre does not often pass over it. There is scarcely a year without the edge of one or more of these fearful storms touching the city; and when the storm-signals proclaim the fact that a cyclone is expected, every one is busy in tying the doors and windows and looking to the fastenings of their houses, so that in case it should come in force they may be safe from its violence. To experience one of these dreadful storms is quite sufficient for a lifetime.

CHAPTER II.

CALCUTTA, THE OXFORD OF INDIA.

CALCUTTA has not inaptly been called the Oxford of India. Having its university and numerous affiliated colleges, it attracts a large number of students from all parts of the province. Some of these belong to the richer families, but the majority of them are poor; nothing is nobler than the sacrifice which many poor Hindus make in order that their sons may obtain a good education. Speaking generally, a man who knows English will rise to a better position and obtain a much higher salary than one who knows Bengali or Hindusthāni only; hence many regard it as a good investment of their money to educate their sons, for it would be most disgraceful were a son who rises in life to retain his income for himself. The picture in *Punch* of a man who, being asked by a lord if his father was present at his table, as he must be proud to see how his son had succeeded, replied, "No, my lord, we must draw the line somewhere!" so far as I know, could never have been given of Hindus. According to a proverbial expression, a man should divide his income into four parts: one goes to the payment of debts, *i.e.* the support of parents; one for current expenses; one for religious purposes; and one is put into the bank, *i.e.* spent in the education of the sons. The Hindu system leads a man to give up his income, whether great or small, to his family; and it often happens that, if a man cannot afford more, he will educate *one* of his sons, the other members of the family, as well

A BENGALI DOCTOR.

as the father, benefiting from the earnings of the educated one.

The University of Calcutta, like that of London, is simply an examining body. It has no teaching staff, but selects the books that are to be read and appoints its examiners. But, by the mere selection of books, it exerts an immense influence upon the thousands of students who attend the colleges. The study of Milton, Shakspeare, &c., has impelled many, who otherwise would probably have never seen it, to carefully read parts of the Bible in order to understand the teachings of these authors. As the University does not teach, a certificate must be obtained by candidates for degrees from one of the colleges affiliated with it that they have attended classes. And before a candidate is sent up for the university examination he must submit to a test examination at his college; so that those only who have a reasonable prospect of passing are allowed to sit for examination. Nearly four thousand students are entered yearly for the matriculation examination at the university, of whom about 45 per cent. pass. After two years comes the First B.A. examination, and after a further course of two years the final B.A.

Great though the desire in England may be to obtain a degree, it is far exceeded in India. A successful candidate has the prospect—now-a-days a faint one in most cases, it is true—of obtaining a situation in a Government office. This is the one thing that is chiefly desired; but though in many offices appointments are obtained by competitive examinations, it is necessary before competing to pass either the Entrance, 1st or 2nd B.A. standard. The same is true of the legal and medical professions. A law or medical student must pass the 1st B.A. examination before he can enter these branches. This forces an immense number of men to work very hard ere they present themselves to the examiners. There is a certain degree of value attached to the fact that a man has been allowed to enter the examinations, although he has failed to pass. It is no uncommon thing to hear a man spoken of as a "failed F.A." or "failed B.A.," *i.e.* one who has been examined for the First Arts or B.A. It shows that he must have matriculated and also have attended the higher classes for two years, and also have passed the test examination of his college. In no country are men more proud of their degrees or more anxious to obtain them than in India. All this has been brought about within the last generation. Educated men, thirty years ago, had no difficulty in obtaining good situations under Government; but now the market is overstocked, and as many who, at great expense have reached what was formerly the open door to honour and a good income, find themselves crowded out they shriek loudly against the Government as though it had acted unfairly towards them. A great deal of the seditious language that finds its way into the native newspapers is the disappointed cry of those who had hoped, on obtaining their degree, to find a straight path to position and wealth. These men have yet to learn that labour is not degrading to an educated man.

The Bengalis are very clever, and avail themselves of any help to get successfully through an examination. For many years the names of examiners were published a year in advance. If they happened to be professors of a Calcutta college, their classes would be crowded with earnest students; if they had published any work, it was eagerly purchased and carefully studied. The peculiarities of their minds were fully noted, and their favourite branches of the subject well attended to. So much was this the case, that of late years it has been the object of the University to keep secret the names of the gentlemen who were to examine, in order that this evil might be avoided.

As there are no residential colleges, the students reside where they like. Many live at home, others in lodgings; whilst for some hostels, as they are called, are opened, *i.e.* houses in which students only reside, and generally those of one caste only, so that they can have their food prepared in strict accord with their religious scruples.

Although there are several centres where the examinations are held, a very large number come to the University building in Calcutta. Sometimes it happens that cholera breaks out amongst the candidates, and in a few hours the hopes of many of the parents are destroyed. Instead of the answers coming into the examiners' hands is a slip with the number of the candidate and one word only, "dead," written upon it. Could those slips speak, what a sad tale they would tell of parents' sacrifice for their children, and of their sadness of heart as they heard of the loss of their sons when it was expected that some return for their years of sacrifice might be made!

So anxious are the students to pass, that it is not at all uncommon for them to appeal to the examiner to give them "passing marks," whether they deserve them or not. As a rule they occupy the whole time allotted for writing; and if unable to answer the questions set, they write something—whether it has anything to do with the questions does not matter. One pleads an attack of fever as a reason for giving in a poor paper; another mentions that he is poor, and if he fail this year all hope of securing his degree is gone. The following authentic copy of a letter will show the style of candidates' appeals:*

"To the Humane Examiner.

"SIR,—Knowing that I shall be plucked in this branch, I am writing an application to show your favor to me. I am a poor man, son of a poor family. But you may say that as I have not worked any single sum how can I show favor towards you. But the reasons. I have passed in the three other days; and I know not why I cannot work these sums; perhaps God is on my opposite side, or my fortune is bad. If you give me ten marks then that will be sufficient for me. If you do not show me this favor I shall lose my whole year. You see distribute pice (money) to poor which is of great labor; but this is of very petty labor, so give me the above-mentioned marks.

"From your most obedient servant."

It will be borne in mind that the examinations of the University are conducted in English. This makes the preparation difficult for boys whose mother-tongue is Bengali, and who scarcely know a word of English until they attend school when they are about eight or nine years of age; but so earnestly do many of them work that, although in conversation they make most numerous and glaring errors, their study of English as a language is far more profound than that of most English-speaking boys. I once examined an English school in Calcutta, in which a few native,

* "Indo-English," p. 71.

mostly Christian, boys were admitted. My paper was on English grammar and composition. I was surprised to find that out of twenty boys, the first, third, fourth, and fifth places were taken by Bengalis. And it often happens in the office examinations, Bengali boys obtain a higher position than English, although in conversation and in the general use of the language they are far behind them.

Calcutta has splendid educational advantages; there are the Government colleges, and the Government aided.

In the Government colleges, all expenses beyond the fees received are paid directly by the Government. For these a splendid staff of professors, graduates of British universities, are provided. As the fees are higher in these than in the aided colleges, the students as a rule come from the more wealthy families; and as many of these students have private tutors to assist them, they generally secure a higher position in the lists. The cost, however, to Government for each student is exceedingly high; and when we remember that most of these students are the sons of rich men, whilst the sum spent by Government on the education of the masses is exceedingly small, a sense of injustice is produced. It is an illustration, though in a sense different from that intended, that "unto him that hath shall be given." These students could well afford to pay much higher fees, and lessen to that extent the cost to the Government; whilst the sum thus liberated might well be spent on the education of the masses.

The Sanskrit College is attended by the sons of the gentry and those of high çaste. A few years ago, when one of the students became a Christian, several of the parents of the other students tried to induce the principal to expel him, who, as they thought, had disgraced his name and family by being baptized. The principal refusing to accede to this cruel request, a petition was presented to the Lieut.-Governor of the province asking him to interfere in the matter. This gentleman very wisely referred the case to a committee of learned men, who, after considerable discussion, declared that they had searched the Hindu scriptures in vain for any prohibition of baptism, and consequently they could adduce no reason why the young man should leave the college. Seeing that the rite of baptism was unknown in India when the old religious books of the Hindus were written, it is not to be wondered at that this decision should have been made. Would that this pronouncement of the committee were generally accepted by the Hindus, that their scriptures do not forbid a man openly declaring himself a Christian—then the great difficulty that the caste system throws in the way of converts would be removed.

After the Government institutions must be mentioned those that receive Government grants. These colleges are worked by the missionaries, or by committees of the natives. A grant-in-aid is given to a college according to the number of its students and the cost of its maintenance. Formerly, similar grants were made to schools; but education has now become so popular in the city that no grants are necessary for them. In the suburbs, however, schools educating up to the entrance standard continue to receive grants in proportion to their expenditure.

There are three Mission colleges in Calcutta, and several others in the province of Bengal. These belong to the General Assembly of the Church of Scotland, the Free Church of Scotland, and the London Missionary Society. In these Institutions over three thousand boys and young men are regularly taught, as they contain schools for the juniors and college classes for the undergraduates. Nearly all the pupils are Hindus. There are a few Christians and Mahomedans, but the Mahomedans, as a rule, keep aloof from the Government and mission schools, and attend their own colleges, where they are taught the Arabic language and the Mahomedan religion.

In addition to the above are colleges and schools supported by the Brahmos and Hindus. These are about equal in value as educational agencies to the mission schools. Many Hindu parents send their sons to them in preference to the Government institutions because their fees are lower, and because morality and religion are taught. Most Hindus believe firmly that education should be religious.

For the European boys there are three institutions, St. Xavier's College, La Martiniere, and the Doveton College. St. Xavier's is well worked by Jesuit professors, and attracts not only Roman Catholics, but also a goodly number of Protestants and Hindus; La Martiniere is almost exclusively for boarders, and is a capital institution for children whose fathers are dead. It has proved an immense boon to many in India. The Doveton College is an endowed school for European and East Indian boys, that does a good work.

For the lower classes there are schools of three grades, in which scholarships may be obtained to enable poorer boys to continue their studies in the colleges; and then, as the lowest of all, come the pātshalas, *i.e.* schools in which the simplest elementary training is given. These were originally *the* schools of India, but they have been quite cast into the shade by the English schools that have so largely superseded them. There is no School Board, but an Educational Department, with its Director of public instruction and inspectors; and it is pleasing to note that the spread of education has been so rapid, that at the present time there is scarely a village that either has not a school of some sort in its midst, or within easy reach of its people. Still, in the improvement of the village schools very much remains to be done, and also in inducing some parents to allow their children to continue at school long enough to obtain sufficient training to make it of use to them. The cruelty of the masters of the old pātshalas was a disgrace to the community; but this is a thing of the past. The birch and cane were mild correctors of youth compared to those once common in India.

From the general education of the people we pass on to notice the provision for training in medicine and surgery. This was *the* need of India. Before the opening of the Medical College, the study and practice of medicine was a very poor affair. Anatomy was out of the question, because by the Hindus it was considered as ceremonially defiling to touch a dead body. The kobirājes, as the ordinary practitioners are called, were a most ignorant set of men. They are still to be seen wandering about with their medicines, ringing a bell to call the attention of the people, and crying their wares as an itinerant cough-lozenge man does in an English market. The peripatetic doctor is a common sight still in the villages, though he is not so frequently seen in the cities. The treatment for diseases of the spleen and liver was certainly heroic. You may see numbers of people with scars as large as a half-crown, where a heated iron has been applied; whilst inoculation for small-pox was most commonly resorted to. There were no schools of medicine: any one who wished could practise, their learning being picked up in a most promiscuous manner. For women there was practically no treatment, as the kobirāj would not be admitted into the women's apartments. In India, Nature, the great healer of disease, has been allowed to have pretty much her own way; and though in many cases she has done well, a little more science and a little more care would have saved the lives of many, and lessened the sufferings of more.

But now this is all changed. There is a splendid medical school at the Medical College, with its large hospital for gaining practical knowledge. At this school the instruction is given in English, and a large number of the students when they have passed their final examinations are employed by the Government to take charge of country districts, in which dispensaries are opened. In order to obtain the degree of M.D., and also admission into the higher grades of the service, it is necessary for the students to come to Great Britain; hence, at the English and Scotch schools of medicine, many of the natives of India are to be found. As, however, the supply of these well-qualified men is not sufficient, or rather as the expense of supporting them for village work is too great, a subordinate class in which instruction is given in the vernacular languages, has been opened, and hundreds of men are under instruction which will qualify them for ordinary practice. Within a few miles of nearly every village, a medical man with a supply of drugs is to be found. This is a great boon, as I can testify. I well remember once being taken seriously ill at a village only thirty miles from Calcutta, where I had to wait about four hours before I could obtain even a little mustard. At the stations where Europeans reside there is always a qualified surgeon, who, in addition to his hospital and dispensary work, has to attend to them. The gentlemen in Government service have a right to his services gratuitously, as his salary is paid by the Government; but when the Government official is married, it is an unwritten law that he gives three days' salary a year to the medical officer for his attendance on his family.

Most astonishing is the progress of education amongst the girls and women. Fifty years ago it was difficult to find a respectable woman who could read. Educated men now prefer educated to ignorant wives, and the standard of female education has gradually risen until the Calcutta University can boast of having had the honour of conferring degrees upon some of the native women of India.

AN ENGLISH DINNER-TABLE IN INDIA.

CHAPTER III.

THE PEOPLE—EUROPEANS IN INDIA.

UPON few questions would opinions be found to differ more than upon this, as to whether for Europeans life is as happy in India as at home. There are some who regard their stay in India as simply exile. Anything at all like England or English customs is gladly welcomed; but to the extent to which the country, the scenery, the people differ from this, they despise and hate them. They count the years, and months—sometimes even the days they have yet to remain there, and hail the time with most intense delight when they can turn their back on India to return no more. But these often find after they have spent some years at home, that "all that glitters is not gold;" that even England is not all that in their absence they had imagined it to be, and sometimes they are inclined to sigh for some of the things that they had enjoyed in India. As a result of this dissatisfaction, life becomes a burden, and it is no wonder if they find many things to annoy them.

Others again, and generally those who enter upon Indian life young, find it to be different indeed in many respects from English, but affording many pleasures that fully compensate for those they have left behind. When the balance is struck, they declare that, on the whole, life is fully as pleasant under the bright skies of India as under the leaden clouds of England; and many who after living a lifetime in India settle down at home, often look back with longing hearts to the land they have left for ever. It is impossible for English people who have never lived in India to enter into the pleasure with which old Indians talk over familiar scenes and congenial pursuits in the sunny East. I shall try to give a fair description of this life, though I do not wish to disguise the fact that I can honestly say, "India, with all thy faults, I love thee still," because, during nearly twenty years there, I had as bright and happy a life as falls to the lot of most men.

The secret of a happy life, whether in England or India, is good health and congenial work. Plenty of work and strength to do it, means happiness in almost any part of the world. That there are many little annoyances in a tropical climate, none can deny; but if the mind is fully occupied with other things, they do not trouble us much. One has only to read the lives of such men as Lord Lawrence, and see them sitting, minus coat and waistcoat, hard at work from morn till night, and we find that under such circumstances the heat that others in other circumstances found most trying was scarcely noticed. I can remember how many a time, when busily engaged, I scarcely noticed that the perspiration was dropping from my chin, and the blotting-pad under my hand was soaking wet, until my attention was called to the fact that it was hot. I can honestly say this, that however hot the temperature might be, I was always able to think; but in England during days of intense cold my brain seemed frozen, and I could do little but shiver and grumble.

As a rule, English gentlemen in India work hard. In the early morning, say about half-past five, they get up, and, after a cup of tea and toast, and fruit, take exercise either on horseback, foot, or cycle. On their return the newspaper comes not wet from the printers, but has dried *en route;* and if he be studious, there is time for an hour's reading. Calcutta boasts of three English daily papers, besides others in English edited by natives. Many in merchants' and some in Government offices bring home work that requires careful attention, and devout an hour or two to this before breakfast. At half-past eight or nine o'clock comes breakfast; but before this is *the* luxury, and also the necessity, of India—the bath. After breakfast there is office work until five or six o'clock, with a short break of about half an hour for tiffin or lunch. On return from office people dine about seven, after which amusement of some kind is sought in the form of reading, cards, billiards, &c. Often, of course, parties are attended and given. There are far more dinner-parties in India than amongst the same classes in England. Except during the cold season there are few public amusements; hence music is more cultivated in the home, and those who have any special talent are well exercised in amateur concerts arranged either for the benefit of the professors of music, or for some local charities. As a rule, English people do not sit up late in India, and with few exceptions they work harder than do many in similar positions at home. I question if any harder-worked class of men could be found than the members of the Indian civil service. Many who have no love for Sunday work declare that it is impossible for them to attend to their routine duties and write the voluminous reports required of them unless they avail themselves of the closing of their offices on Sundays.

But with the English ladies, life certainly presents a different aspect. Whilst husband and sons are at office, the days must appear terribly long to those at home, because during half the year at least, in the belief that by this means the heat is lessened, the light is almost excluded. A stranger arriving in India in the hot season is greatly astonished at the general paleness of the ladies. It is not that they are all ill, but, living in semi-darkness for months together, they look washed out, just as plants that are kept in darkness. The Indian houses are constructed on quite an opposite plan from that of our English homes. Here we want snugness and warmth; in India coolness and air: so that whilst the windows in English houses are made with the intention of being occasionally opened; in India they are made with the intention of being occasionally closed. The glass sashes are fitted with hinges, and closed when it rains, or during the hot part of the day to exclude the heated air. Outside of these are the thick

DOOR OF HOUSE, SHOWING SASHES AND VENETIANS.

Venetians; made of three-quarter inch wood, with flaps about three inches wide. These are arranged so that they can be closed, or left half open. In the hot season about 9 a.m. these Venetians and the glass sashes are closed, so that only a little light can enter the rooms. When, therefore, a lady remains indoors from 9 a.m. until 5 p.m. with only household and family duties to occupy her mind, it is not to be wondered at that she finds life somewhat dull. But when, as in many cases they are now attempting it, they go out for school work, or visiting, their minds and hands being occupied they have not the same monotonous existence that was so distressing.

AN AYAH.

The most noticeable thing in Anglo-Indian society is the absence of young people. In almost every family there are sad hearts and anxious minds because of the absence of the children, who have been sent home at an early age, and from whom a long separation is inevitable. As a rule, up to seven or eight years of age, children thrive as well in India as at home; but after that time they visibly droop, and for their physical as well as mental and moral good, it is necessary that they should be sent to a more congenial clime.

As an illustration of the necessity of sending children home may be mentioned the fact that it is almost impossible to make them self-helpful and self-reliant in India. Servants are numerous, and very submissive. I have often been amused, and at the same time pained, to see boys walking to school with a servant in attendance to carry their books. Boys having servants within call can with the greatest difficulty be taught to do anything for themselves. On moral grounds, the necessity for sending the children away is greater still. Boys cannot be trained to become truthful and fearless in the cowardly and untruthful atmosphere of India. If a child does wrong, the servants will deliberately lie in the very presence of the child, and thus show that lying saves from punishment. No amount of good instruction can counteract this.

There are few husbands who have not passed through the painful experience of putting wife and children on board a steamer, and then going back to an empty house that had before resounded with children's voices. This is *the one* unutterably painful experience of life in the East. At some time or other the hour of decision comes to most married people; who must make the sacrifice, husband or children? Must the wife go and remain at home with the children whilst the husband lives alone; or must the children be left in England without a home for years. Bitter has been the experience of children thus left behind. I have heard of some, for whose education and comfort large fees have been paid, being half starved, badly taught, and made little better than domestic drudges by those who ought honestly to have treated them well: and all this time the children were compelled to write to their parents elaborately false statements speaking of the kindness they received, and of the comforts they enjoyed. When children thus treated in their turn become parents, and their children are too old to remain in India, they determine that, whatever happens, their children shall never suffer in this manner. To prevent this the mother remains in England for years, whilst the father toils on in loneliness, with the satisfaction that he is doing the best he can for his children. Many English families in India have thus been broken up for many years together.

Those who have never been called to part with their children cannot at all realize the position of parents in India. After a letter has come by the mail, telling of the dangerous illness of a beloved child, a long week must elapse before any further tidings can be received: and the parents know that were they to start off home at once, long before they could reach their loved one their help would come too late. Before the telegraphic communication was made, this was far worse than it is at present. But even with the telegraph the trial is very hard to bear; the utter helplessness one feels to do anything for those dearer than life itself cannot be described.

A sad chapter might be written on the romance of Anglo-Indian life: a chapter, though chiefly in a tragic vein, would not be without its comedy too. As illustrations of the tragic side of life, the following may be given; and a goodly number of similar stories might easily be told. A wife and family start from England to rejoin the husband and father. They have been separated for years; the one bright star has been the hope of seeing and being welcomed back by him who was the constant topic of thought and conversation on the voyage. The imagination had painted the happy meeting, the joy of talking together of events that had happened during the separation. The ship drops anchor, and when the voyagers are eagerly looking for the smiling face of the one so dear, a friend comes with the sad story that he is dead. Or, again, a husband in the solitude of his Indian home, instead of the welcome weekly letter from his wife, sees a letter in a stranger's writing. As he tremblingly opens it, he finds that his wife has gone, and that the happy meeting he had hoped for will never be in this world. And parents hearts' are almost broken as they receive the news that the child from whom they have been parted for years, and whom they were hoping to see soon as bright sunshine in their home, has been taken from them. When we are with our dear ones and see their gradual decline, and with sympathizing heart and loving hand have done all we could to alleviate their sufferings, death is painful; but the suddenness of the blow as it falls upon the bereaved in a distant country, makes it very heavy to bear. Occasionally it happens even now, when passengers travel quickly in steamers—but in the days when they came round the Cape it was a more frequent occurrence—that young men on going down to meet their intended brides have found that, on the voyage, their heart's affection had been transferred to a fellow-passenger, and the faithful one has had to return to his friends to receive condolences on his loss instead of congratulation on his bliss. Sometimes it happens that a gentleman, not seeing any one in India he cared to marry, and not being in a position to go home to seek a bride, has made love by letter to a friend of a friend, and when the lady arrived he has needed an introduction to her who in a day or two would become his bride. But these experiences have become rare since the journey has been reduced from one hundred and twenty to thirty days.

Another feature of Anglo-Indian life is the great hospitality that is shown to strangers. Certainly in this matter things are managed better there than here. When a gentleman or lady arrives in India, it is not the custom for them to wait until the residents happen to hear of their arrival, but bringing a letter of introduction, or perhaps knowing some one in the place, they soon find friends to welcome them. They first inquire on whom they should call. Within a week the visit is returned, and probably within a month they will be invited to dine at the houses of a good number of those on whom they have called. In this manner they soon feel at home though living in a new country. It is a custom of the country coming down from the good old times when people kept almost open house, for an extra plate and knife and fork to be always placed on the dinner-table. The servants do it without an order, so that if a guest come in there is a chair ready for him. In country stations where there are no hotels, it is not uncommon for a traveller to be commended to the care of a resident through a mutual friend, though host and guest have never met; nor is it unusual for a perfect stranger to write to ask for entertainment for a day or two. Accustomed as we are to the hotel system of Europe, it is a pleasant surprise to meet with the hospitality that is so common in India; and old Indians returning to England, contrast the friendliness of India with the coldness of England in this matter.

Another peculiarity of Anglo-Indian life is the freedom of intercourse between Europeans. In England I have been astonished to see gentlemen who have been associated in politics and Christian work for years address each other as "Mr." Smith and "Mr." Brown; and in speaking, say "Sir" to each other, as though they were new acquaintances. But this is very rare in India. "Sir" is seldom used, and gentlemen within a few minutes of being introduced to each other drop the "Mr.," and address each other by their surnames. Of course all Englishmen are not regarded as equals. There is a line separating them into two great classes—those in society and those outside; *i.e.* those who have the privilege of appearing at the *levée* of the Governor-General, and those who have not this privilege. Within this sacred enclosure all are theoretically equal—or at any rate they associate in many things on equal terms; but between those within and those without this charmed circle there is not much sympathy. In certain places in England there is a rigid line separating society from the rest; but I have never heard in England of exclusiveness such as prevails in Anglo-Indian society. Clerks in merchants' offices may appear at Government House, but the heads of the large tradesmen's houses are excluded, though some of the latter are quite as well educated, and as gentlemanly in their character and life, as some of the former. In the small stations where there are from ten to twenty Government officials, in social gatherings and outside of office all meet on pretty nearly equal terms; but the subordinates whose position does not entitle them to bow to the representative of the Queen are left out in the cold. It cannot but be exceedingly painful to many whose character and education are equal to the best, to find themselves, by the rigid rules of society, cut off from friendly intercourse with their neighbours.

In English homes in India, as in other respects, there is a growing tendency to assimilate India to England—sometimes, as it appears to me, to an unwise extent. Were it not for the punkah swaying to and fro over our head, and the presence of dark-skinned servants, when in Calcutta, one might often imagine oneself in a home in England. English carpets are hiding the clean and neat-looking mats that were once universal. Stencilled patterns on the walls above the darker dado are becoming common instead of the whitewashed or simply tinted walls. Ordinary dishes are supplanting the once loved curries and kedgeri, or rice and dhall (a kind of pulse) boiled together. Ladies seeing the *Queen* and other books of fashion only three weeks after they are published, do not wait, as many do in the county towns of England, to see some of the more forward adapt the newest style, but at once go to the extreme, lest by the time they have had their dresses made the fashion should again change. Far more commonly than was the case a few years ago, in the evening gentlemen parade in the abomination of modern society, the chimney-pot hat; though at present, excepting new arrivals, gloves are not commonly worn by them. It is amusing to see in old pictures, Indian missionaries wearing the dress coat and silk hat when preaching under a tree to a crowd of semi-nude Hindus. This certainly is not the mode at present in vogue. During the hot season men of all classes wear white trousers, not because they are cool, but because they are clean, and thin tweed jackets. During the day, all sensible men who have to go out into the open air wear helmets of pith or cork.

I am decidedly of opinion that in eating and drinking most Europeans act very unwisely. In a climate where temperance in both these respects is called for, and where there is an abundance of vegetables and fruit of many kinds, there is intemperance. It is my firm conviction that a great many who fall victims, as they think to the climate, really fall victims to their own foolishness. Many English people have three heavy meals in the day. At breakfast there is fish, chops, cutlets, omelets, eggs, toast, &c.; at tiffin (lunch) there are chops, steaks, curry and rice, puddings, &c.; at dinner in the evening a long course concludes the day's work. As to drinking, there is even greater foolishness. Many in the hot season take beer at breakfast and tiffin, with pegs (*i.e.* brandy and soda-water) between, and in the evening beer, spirits, wine. Many gentlemen, who would feel insulted if you hinted that they were not temperate, take half a bottle of spirits a day, in addition to beer, &c. I am speaking not of drunkards, but of those who through the habitual use of these things take as much as I have mentioned without apparently being any the worse for it. It is sad to see young men drawn into a society where such customs prevail. There is not much drinking in hotels or public houses; but there is a great deal in private houses and in "chummeries," as they are called—*i.e.* houses where single gentlemen live together. These are very numerous in Calcutta. Four or more gentlemen take a house and have a set of servants to cater for them; no housekeeper being required, as the head servant (khansamah) exercises a general control over the food, &c., and the sirdar bearer, the head bearer or house servant, takes charge of the house. Where a steady set live together, this is a comfortable arrangement for bachelors; but where they are not steady, this style of living proves most hurtful to character.

The climate of Calcutta calls for a word of notice. Formerly it was called the "grave of Europeans." Years ago, when a student in a civil service class asked the teacher why promotion was more rapid in Bengal than in any other province, the answer was very simple: "Because there are more deaths there." But it seems to me that it is a case of "giving a dog a bad name and then hanging him." The ordinary death-rate is not usually higher than it is in many towns in England; but this statement needs the qualification that a good many are sent away who die on the passage, or soon after their arrival at home, whilst nearly all Europeans leave before they grow very old. But I believe that a good part of the mortality of Europeans can be clearly traced to the intemperance I have spoken of above.

The year is naturally divided into three seasons—the cold, hot, and rainy seasons. For three months, *i.e.* from the middle of November to the middle of February, the climate is simply perfect. The sky is bright and cloudless, whilst a cool fresh wind is almost constantly blowing. During these months the air acts as a splendid tonic, so that after a few days the weakness and weariness of the rainy season are almost forgotten. Though the season is called cold, it must not be imagined that it is at all like an English winter. During the day the thermometer rises to about 70°, but in the early morning it falls to about 56°. After a few years' residence in India, the body becomes weakened and the pores of the skin so open, owing to the excessive perspiration, that one can enjoy the comfort of an overcoat, and occasionally the cheerful heat of a fire. In most houses in Calcutta there are no fireplaces; but where there is one, a fire will be lighted for about a fortnight in January. As I was a fortunate person in this respect, in order to enjoy the semblance of home-life on Christmas and New Year's Eve we lighted a fire, and the first year or two after our arrival in India opened the glass sashes to make the fire bearable; but after a few years we could enjoy the fire even with closed windows.

Following the cold comes the hot season, *i.e.* from February 15th to June 15th. During these months the thermometer registers from 85 to 105 degrees. This is rather too warm; but as Calcutta is only

5

about ninety miles from the seas, when the sun goes down a sea breeze springs up, so that, unlike the inland country, the nights are generally bearable. During this season we have frequent storms, "Nor'-westers" as they are termed. After a perspiring day we see a most clearly marked, semicircular cloud gather, and in a short time it is on us. Doors and windows are carefully closed, because before the rain, which is so welcome, falls, dense clouds of dust come—so dense, in fact, that one cannot see the horse's head from the vehicle if we are caught when driving. But the cool and fresh feeling of the atmosphere as the rain comes down in torrents must be realized in order to know what is meant by "cooling showers in a desert land." Although the heat is great, it is generally remarked that Europeans enjoy better health in the hot than during the cold season.

From June 15th to November 15th is the rainy season. For the first month or so the rains are welcomed because of the new life that is seen in the gardens, and for the pleasant fall in the temperature. During these weeks slight showers only fall, and the atmosphere is not saturated with moisture; but during July and August the rains come in earnest. It is not a continuous downpour; black clouds and a heavy rainfall alternate with bright and sunny skies. By the beginning of September the ground is like a soaked sponge, and as the rains moderate and the sun beats upon the earth, the malaria rises, and the atmosphere is like a vapour-bath. Collars are limp before they can be fastened. Perspiration exudes from every pore of the skin, but the atmosphere is too moist to absorb it. The backs of books take leave of the bodies, and the paper feels damp and sodden. Boots taken off at night are covered with green mould before morning. The most enthusiastic admirer of India cannot say much in favour of the climate during this time. Mark Tapley would have found it hard to be jolly during October in Calcutta. It is the season for fever, dysentery, &c., and other cruel diseases. Happily it soon passes away, and with the beginning of November the wind occasionally blows from the N.W., and as this increases in force, it drives away the hot and moist atmosphere which has been trying the health and temper of the luckless souls who have been compelled to vegetate in the plains. As an instance of the regularity of the seasons, I may just note that I have known for three years in succession the first rain to fall about twelve o'clock at noon of the 15th of June, the nominal date of the commencement of this season.

It is customary for Europeans to arrive in India during the cold season, and nothing appears to surprise them more than the continued sunshine. As friends fresh from England who have been my guests have greeted me with the commonplace remark, "What a beautiful morning!" I have allowed it to pass for a few days, and then have gently hinted that the same remark would hold good for months to come. I have known some whose whole frame seemed so excited with this superlative brightness that they could scarcely get to sleep at night. Lest, however, some should imagine that India at this season is absolutely perfect, I may mention the fact that we have at times terribly heavy fogs, and that at this season, too, musquitos are both more numerous and more vicious than during any other part of the year. Even India provides some drawbacks to its many excellences.

WATER-CARRIERS.

In a description of European life in India, a word must be said about servants. Upon this question there is as great diversity of opinion as on the same question in every land. Moving about in this country, one hears a great deal said about the increasing difficulty of obtaining good servants; and the correspondence in the newspapers indicates a widespread sense of dissatisfaction. On the other hand, there are those who speak most gratefully of faithful service, and manifest the deepest interest in and affection for their servants. Precisely the same experience is found in India. There are some people who have not a good word for the servant class. They say they are lazy, dirty, untruthful, dishonest. And such people speak the absolute truth so far as their experience goes. But it is not by any means the whole truth. The servants of Europeans come from the lowest classes; and in a city like Calcutta are many who cannot get employment in small places, where their antecedents are known. And further, the natives cling together, and speak freely of their employers. When therefore it is known that a master or mistress is unkind, harsh, inconsiderate, cruel, the better class of servants will not serve them. But, on the other hand, there are servants as clean, honest, kind, and industrious as one could wish them to be. From what I have seen I can say that I could not wish to be better served than I have been for many years by most of the men who have been in my employment. It is true that if a servant does not wish to do certain work because he considers it does not properly belong to his position, he will plead that his caste forbids him to do it, whereas frequently his caste does nothing of the kind. On the other hand, it is perfectly true that some Europeans, through ignorance, indifference, or selfishness, will order their servants to do work which they would rather starve than do; and these nominally Christian masters will beat a servant for not doing what he believes his religion positively forbids. Where masters are fairly kind and thoughtful, there are many servants to be found who are really trustworthy and faithful.

A BENGALI WASHERMAN.

The great bone of contention between masters and servants is what is known in India as "dustoori," and in England as commission. It is part of the Bengali servant's creed that it is his privilege, his undoubted right, to obtain a percentage out of every rupee that his master spends. And, as a rule, they succeed in getting it. The master calls it "stealing;"

the servant says, "No, I am not a thief, though I take my dustoori." Men who would not on any account steal in the ordinary use of the word, will claim this commission. But there are others who doubtless will steal, and that very cleverly. It is a common custom with those who are most anxious to have pure milk, for the cow to be brought to the door of the house to be milked, and for one of the family to stand by to see the operation. The man will hold his brass milk pail upside down to show that it is empty; but if the watcher's back is turned but for a moment, out comes a wet cloth that was round the milkman's waist, and the filthy water it contained is wrung into the milk vessel. I have known many such tricks as this resorted to, which go to prove that however careful an Englishman may be, he will most certainly be outwitted in the long run by the intelligent natives of India. On the other hand, where there is anything approaching kindly feeling manifested, good and pure milk can be purchased; and, from many, true and faithful service obtained. I can say that, as far as my personal experience is concerned, I have had as good and trustworthy servants in India as in England.

When people unfamiliar with India hear of the large number of servants in an Anglo-Indian house, they imagine that luxurious and costly living is the rule. But this is by no means the case. A set of about eight Indian servants do the work of two in England, and cost little if any more. As the cookroom is always at a little distance from the house, so that the heat and smell may be avoided, ladies seldom enter it; and the servants mostly live at their own homes, or in rooms quite separate from the house in which they serve. A cook-room in a house where the doors leading to the different rooms are always open would be an intolerable nuisance. Excepting Christian āyahs, or nurses, the servants not only live out of the house, but also provide their own food, so that the low salary paid to them covers all the expense connected with them. Strange to say, there

COOK IN THE COOK-ROOM.

are few Calcutta-born people who act as servants to Europeans;—they come from Orissa and the north-western province of India, work for a couple of years or so, and then pay a visit of a few months to their wives and families. When away on leave they secure a substitute; and it is a point of honour with the substitute, however much the master may desire it, not to remain when the old servant returns.

CHAPTER IV.

THE PEOPLE GENERALLY.

We now pass on to describe the people generally who are included under the general title *native.* It is hard to say why this word should be so commonly used, since all of us are natives of some place or other; but as the term is used in a somewhat disparaging sense, it is not to be wondered at that the educated Bengalis should sometimes resent it. Our Christians seldom speak of themselves as *native* Christians, but rather as Bengali Christians—certainly a far more appropriate and respectful appellation.

In appearance many of the Bengalis are exceedingly like Europeans. There is no doubt whatever that the higher castes, who have not intermarried with the aborigines whom they found in India, and of whose country they took possession, belong to the great Aryan family;—their language, mythology, customs, all point to a common ancestry with that of the branches of this great family in Europe, as the Greeks, Italians, Germans, Celts, &c. Frequently I have noticed faces exactly like those of people in England. The lower castes who for the most part are a mixed race, being the descendants of the Hindus and the original inhabitants of the country, differ more widely from the European type. But if any one expects to find people at all approaching the

A GROUP OF THE NATIVES OF INDIA.

negro, he must not go to India for them. He will find as many or perhaps more in London or Liverpool than he will in Calcutta. And yet many English people continually speak to and of the natives of India as *niggers*, when in truth they are no more like "niggers" than themselves. To those who know well and love the Bengalis, it is most painful to see the contempt that some Europeans seem to cherish for them.

In colour there is perhaps greater diversity than in England. The highest type of beauty of complexion in Bengal is "golden." Lakshmi, the goddess of prosperity, and Durgā, the favourite goddess of the province, are always represented, whether in pictures or images, as having a bright, gold-coloured skin. And this is the colour of the higher castes who have not been much exposed to the sun. I have seen many far fairer than the olive-tinted Italians who wander through our streets, discoursing sweet music from their organs. Others, again, are of an olive tint; and others, mostly of the lower castes, are very dark. But though their hair is black it is never woolly, and, as a rule, the skin is so beautifully smooth and transparent that one might imagine they were accustomed from their birth to use Pears' wonderful soap, or were made "beautiful for ever" by Madame Rachel's marvellous method. "Golden" is one of the many names or epithets of Durgā; and much as we pride ourselves on our fair skin, the Bengali wife would not at all like her children to be white. It is not so much because the negroes are black that they are objects of terror to our little ones, as the fact that they are unaccustomed to them, and because the threat of "a black man coming" is used to frighten them. When an English child arrives in Calcutta, if it has not seen the native āyahs on board, it shrinks with the utmost terror from them, exactly in the same manner as I have seen Bengali children scream and kick to get away from my white face. But when they become familiar with their dark faces, they are more ready to go to them than to a strange white-faced person.

The dress of the people is most various, but it is a capital indication of the nationality, and often the religious position, of its owner. The poor people generally wear white calico; the men have two strips, each about two and a half yards long, one of which, the dhuti, is for the loins, the other, the chādar, for the upper part of the body; the women have one long strip of five and a half yards, called a sāri. In the hot season the men use the chādar as a turban, leaving the upper part of the body exposed; the women fasten the sāri round their waist, and then bring the remainder over the head. It cannot be said that this is altogether a decent dress, as one side of the breast is generally exposed; and when the wind happens to blow, the light material is carried with it, leaving the body rather too much undraped. The borders of these strips of calico are generally coloured; but the widows cannot wear a coloured border. The coolies in the streets altogether dispense with the chādar, and are content to wear only the cloth round their loins. The clerks and middle classes usually wear a chapkan, a garment somewhat like a frock coat, fastened on the side of the breast. A Hindu can at once be distinguished from a Mussulmān, as the Hindu tucks his dhuti on the right-hand side, and the Mussulmān on the left. An amusing story may be told, illustrating the power of clothes, and also showing that, after all, there is a good deal in a name. A Christian convert in Government employ, anxious to obtain a higher post in his office, was told that it could not be given to a Bengali, but

COOLIE (LABOURER) WAITING FOR HIRE.

was reserved for a European. "If that is all, and I am otherwise fit for it," he said, "I will be a European." So off he went to a tailor, and was rigged out in European costume, and at the same time he gave himself an Anglicized form of his Bengali name. After this change of dress and name he obtained the appointment, and he held it until his death, which happened a few years ago. Though the ordinary dress of the Bengali gentleman consists of white trousers and a chapkān, made of some quiet-coloured alpaca or tweed, on festival days he adorns himself in the gayest colours of silk and satin. Bright blues, greens, scarlets, and yellows are not at all too striking for these occasions. The Hindus have yet to learn that the gay plumage which adorns the males of the animal world, and which the dandies of uncivilized countries still affect, amongst the more civilized peoplos is a monopoly of the ladies.

As a rule the Hindus do not wear shoes or stockings; but amongst the educated classes there is a nondescript kind of dress coming into fashion that is neither European nor Asiatic, but a mixture of both. They frequently wear the ordinary loose dhuti for trousers, and an English shirt, not tucked in, for the chādar;—a white shirt in summer and a coloured flannel one in the cold season. They also wear stockings and shoes. Stockings are all right when the trousers hide the upper part, but they certainly look very strange on men whose legs are exposed from the knees, and when the garters are openly displayed. A story is told of a certain Chief Justice of Calcutta who was greatly scandalized as he saw the naked legs and unshod feet of his dusky brethren in the streets. Turning to a learned brother who had come to meet him at the ship which had brought him from England, he said: "We must certainly try to improve all this." I fear this good man's sympathetic nature would be disturbed were he to revisit India to-day, to find that after the lapse of so many years the people generally go barefooted as of old. The greatest innovation, I think, that can be pointed out, is the almost universal use of umbrellas. English manufacturers must have made a good thing out of our connection with India, as annually many

A BRÂHMAN IN SECULAR EMPLOYMENT.

thousands of these articles are imported, all classes of the community now seeming to regard an umbrella as a necessity. At the commencement of the rainy season the servants put in a claim for a new umbrella, the article that once was the exclusive luxury of the rich and in some districts the sign of royalty. It is a question for the curious, What becomes of the old umbrellas? Like pins and donkeys, they have a most mysterious power of suffering annihilation.

Certainly no people on earth are prouder of jewellery than the Hindu and Mahomedan ladies; and the gentlemen seem pleased that their wives should have this means of adornment, though they can be seen by few except the members of their own family. There are jewels for the hair, forehead, nose, ears, arms, wrists, waist, fingers, ankles, and toes; and some exceedingly beautiful ornaments have been designed. Although from their size and weight the anklets must be very burdensome as they walk, yet the poor women who work as carriers of bricks and mortar for the bricklayers are not at all behind their sisters who are immured in the recesses of the Zenāna khannah. In former days families invested their savings in jewellery; and to show their possessions to a stranger is one of the great delights of the Hindu ladies. It is a most pretty sight to see Hindu girls at a gala day at school, dressed in their gay-coloured robes, whilst their bodies are laden with jewels.

The people are divided into a great number of castes or classes, who, though they may speak and work together, will not visit each other, nor eat or drink together. These distinctions originated hundreds, if not thousands, of years ago, and a more complete system of gradations in society it would be difficult to conceive. Originally there were four great classes—(1) The Brāhmans, or priestly class; (2) the Kshatriya, or soldier caste; (3) the Vaishya, or merchant class; and (4) the Sudra, or servant class. The three highest castes are said to be twice-born, and are allowed to wear the poitra, *i.e.*

a little necklace of thread, of which all who wear it are exceedingly proud; but the main object in life of the Sudras is to serve the others, and they are taught that it is an honour for them to be allowed to put the dust from a Brāhman's foot upon their head, or to drink the water in which he has washed his feet. No poor ignorant Roman Catholic pays so great deference to his priest as the low-caste man in India pays to the Brāhman. Formerly the Brāhmans were allowed only to do the work of priests, and attend to religious duties in the temples; but now they are clerks, schoolmasters, and merchants. A more proud race of men it would be hard to find.

All the Hindus do not hold the same religious views: thero are sects differing quite as much in doctrine and practice as the Roman Catholic differs from the Brethren in England. Most of these sects wear distinctive marks on their foreheads or in their dress, so that one who has studied this question can tell at a glance whether a man is a worshipper of Siva or Vishnu, and also within these large divisions the particular sect of which he is a member. There are some who hold that God is a Spirit, and that it is wrong to make any image of Him; yet these same men, though in private they ridicule the idolatrous and superstitious practices of their fellow Hindus, do not scruple to perform religious ceremonies in front of an image, or to teach the people to worship idols. It is in India to-day as it was with the philosophers of Rome, who, when in private, ridiculed the gods, yet taught the people to respect and reverence them. All the people, however, are Pantheists—*i.e.* they believe that God is everything and everything is God; hence some of them say in excuse of such sins as lying, stealing, &c., "We are parts of God, and only speak the words and do the deeds to which He impels us. We cannot be, we cannot do other than we are and do."

Then there are the Mussulmāns, the followers of the great teacher Mahomed, who rose in Arabia, and who, by his teaching and the use of the sword, brought a large part of Asia and Europe to embrace his religion. These men are most bigoted. They hold that as the New Testament, being later than the Old, contains a fuller revelation of God, the Korān, being later than the New Testament, contains still fuller light than its predecessor. The position of the Christian teacher with them is very much the same as would be that of a Jew were he to try to lead back Christians to Judaism. Their reverence for Mahomed is quite as great as is the reverence of Christians for Jesus Christ.

In addition to the Hindus who are devoted to the worship of idols, and the Mahomedans who regard idolatry as the greatest sin, there are many educated men who have given up Hinduism, but have not embraced Christianity. These are generally regarded as Brahmos, *i.e.* men who acknowledge one supreme God, but do not seek for any mediator between themselves and Him. Their religion consists in reading the Bible and other religious books, such as the older Hindu scriptures. They meet regularly for worship, and in many of their sermons it would be difficult for a stranger to see wherein they differ from Christians. These men dress as Hindus, and many of them are as scrupulous about eating with men of other castes as though they were ordinary Hindus. In addition to all these, there are the Parsis, or Fire-worshippers from Persia, who, when their country was conquered by the Mahomedans, took refuge in India. There are a good number of Jews, many of whom retain their peculiar dress, and whilst speaking the language of the people amongst whom they live, also learn Hebrew at their schools. They remain a distinct class in India as in England.

In a large city like Calcutta we have a number of people from all parts of the country. For example, when the new trade of pipe-laying for gas and water had to be done, Oriyas from Orissa came in, and not a single Bengali is engaged in this work. For road-making and for sweeping the streets, some of the aboriginal tribes from Santālia and other hill districts have been induced to settle in the city, whilst the servants either come from the North-West Provinces or from Orissa. As it is contrary to a Hindu's religious notions to touch beef, and in fact most of the food eaten by Europeans, the cooks and servants who wait at table, with a very few exceptions, are Mahomedans. The tailoring and dressmaking, the bricklaying and painting work, is also done by Mahomedans. As the Hindus follow the trades and callings of their ancestors, they could not take kindly to any new form of industry. Men who were free from these caste prejudices have therefore had a decided advantage over them.

A very common libel on the Bengalis is that they are dirty. As far as my observation goes, I do not know any people more cleanly in their habits. As a rule, the Hindus bathe every day of the year, and as soon as they have bathed they wash the clothes they have worn the last twenty-four hours, which, when dry, are ready to wear the next day. If there is a river within a reasonable distance, the people prefer to bathe in it, because a bath in a river not only cleanses their bodies, but is believed also to wash away their sins. If there is no river convenient, they bathe in a tank; or if this cannot be had, they pour water over their bodies. They do not use soap, but in the cold season, immediately before their

GRINDING CORN.

bath, anoint the body with cocoa-nut oil. If soon after this ceremony they crowd into a room, the smell of oil is rather strong than pleasant. Their cooking vessels and brass plates and dishes are scrupulously clean. Hinduism has certainly taught the people cleanliness, which is said to be next to godliness.

For the most part the Hindus are vegetarians. In Bengal they live on rice and vegetables made into a sort of stew with hot spices, which is known to English people as curry. Those who can afford it take fish, though some Hindus are so scrupulous that they will not even eat fish, because it involves the destruction of life. Occasionally they eat a little goat's flesh or venison. When a goat has been sacrificed to Kāli it becomes sacred, and a Hindu then may freely eat it; but as the people are mostly very poor, they cannot afford often to indulge in this luxury. It is for some religious purpose that a goat is sacrificed, as the fulfilment of a vow when a son is born, or when there has been recovery from illness, or some special benefit obtained. Of late years, however, religious butchers have appeared. In their shops is an image, or in some cases a picture, of Kāli, before which the animals are slain. This simple process sanctifies the meat, and the people who could not purchase a whole kid can buy a pound or two of this holy meat and eat it. As a rule the people are teetotalers too. Lately, as greater facilities have been given them for procuring spirits, the number of drinkers has greatly increased. It is a cruel shame that a Christian Government should assist in the moral injury of its subjects. But it is only too true that spirit-shops are much more numerous than they were; and it is equally certain that if the people generally were consulted they would close all, or nearly all, that are now open. Once in my house a meeting was held to protest against the granting of a spirit license, on the ground that there were four others within a very short distance. The collector heard all we had to say, and granted the license next day.

In eating their food, though the right hand takes the place of knife and fork and a spoon, the people are very clean and careful. Before commencing a meal the hands are carefully washed; and though it may appear strange to us, they consider our plan of using spoons, &c., that have been in the mouths of other people, although they have been washed, extremely dirty. Their carefulness in the matter of eating goes rather to scrupulosity. If a servant is called when eating his food, he will send a message, "I am eating my dinner," as though this were a sufficient excuse for not coming at once. If, however, the matter is urgent, and he is ordered to come, he will obey; but the uneaten food is thrown away, lest perchance any one of another caste should have gone near it in the interval. Whilst preparing and cooking their food they are equally careful. If any one crosses the line which they have drawn around them, the food is defiled; and when the vessels are made of earthenware, they are all broken up. I fail to see where the truthfulness of the charge of "dirtiness" can be laid against the Hindu. At a meal where several persons are present, or when a feast is given, the dishes of food are placed on the ground, and each takes out with his hands what he requires.

After a meal it is most common for the people to eat pān, as it is called. This is a leaf grown specially for the purpose, in which betel-nut, lime, cinnamon, cardamums, and other spices are mixed, the whole being fastened together with a clove. This produces the redness of the lips that is so noticeable amongst them. It is rather repulsive to see this red juice on the face; and it is considered disrespectful for a servant to enter the house with this stuff in his mouth. It seems to me that the frequent use of hot spices is called for by the nature of their food. They have to eat an immense quantity of rice in order to obtain a sufficiency of nutriment. As rice forms their staple food every day in the year, and they have no change of diet to stimulate the appetite or to assist in digestion, these condiments seem to be necessary. Their contentment with this simple and changeless diet is astonishing.

When the people meet each other, or when a European meets with them, except they have become familiar with our customs, there is no hand-shaking as a sign of friendliness. In fact, many of the old orthodox Hindus would decidedly object to shake hands with us. When they meet as equals, each touches his forehead with the palm of the right hand; but if an inferior meet a superior, he stoops down as though he would touch the foot of the other, and then slowly raises it to his head. They mean by this just what we do by the shake of the hands. But after this is over, one has to be very careful how we ask questions about the family. If we have heard that a gentleman's wife is ill, it would be a great breach of etiquette to ask after her by name. Although we know he has no children, if we wish to learn anything about his wife we have to say, "How is your family?" This he at once understands, and will tell you she is better or worse, as the case may be. Strange to say, in the Bengali, and as far as I know in all other Indian languages, there is no word for "Thank you." When a service is rendered it is possible to express the pleasure the service has given, but the fact remains that there is no word to express the idea of gratitude. On one occasion, as a translator was seated with his pundit trying to get a word for gratitude, when at last the pundit had taken in the idea that was in the gentleman's mind, he said, "Sir, what there is not in a country, how can there be a name for it!" Owing to this fact, when servants and others do anything for an Englishman's comfort, he has to take it as a matter of course, without the word of thanks that is common amongst ourselves.

In terminating a visit from a Bengali gentleman, there is rather a strange form of etiquette into which Europeans do not easily fall, viz., the visitor does not rise to go until his host has politely informed him that it is time for him to take his departure. Ignorant of this custom, or from past habit strongly disinclined to it, English gentlemen have allowed a Bengali visitor to remain for two or three hours—the one hoping the other would leave, the other as earnestly hoping that he would soon be dismissed, the politeness of host and guest preventing either from making a move. It is as polite in Bengal to tell your visitor that the time has come for him to retire, as the same action would be the opposite of polite in England. One has only to travel a little to see the truth of the old adage, "Many men, many customs."

In an assembly, or a crowded street, the respect that is almost universally shown to an Englishman is most marked. As a rule a passage will be made for him, even though this means the greater discomfort of those around. And the reason why a European missionary often attracts a greater congregation than a Bengali Christian in the street, arises largely from the fact that the people are pleased to hear a foreigner talking in their own language. It has often surprised me to see the universal respect that is shown to a man who is stammering in their language, and probably making a blunder in every sentence. Not a smile crosses their faces, nor does the speaker know from the appearance of his hearers that he is not speaking with the greatest elegance and correctness. I was once seated next a gentleman who intended to ask a servant to pour some water into his tumbler; instead of which he really asked the man to put him into the glass. The water, however, was given, and not so much as the ghost of a smile was on the servant's face. I dare say behind our backs great fun is had at our expense; but in our presence there is not the slightest sign of it.

There is, generally speaking, no humour in the Bengali. Life is too real, too stern a matter for laughter. If an order has to be given, it must be given in the plainest language. A missionary once took a country lad as a servant when going out on a boating journey. As there are no lavatories on board these country boats, one's ablutions have to be performed in a very simple manner, an ordinary bucket serving as wash-bowl. The lad was ordered to bring some water, and in doing so happened to spill a little on the floor. The missionary said, "Why do you not throw it all over me?" "Aha," said the lad, and immediately took up the pail and emptied it over the missionary's head, to that gentleman's astonishment. The lad could not see the humour in the speech, and was astonished to find that words are not always used to express the same idea.

A BATHING-PLACE PROTECTED FROM ALLIGATORS.

CHAPTER V.

A TALK ABOUT INSECTS, REPTILES, ETC.

In India and tropical countries generally, one seems to be in nature's wholesale establishment, where her transactions are on a large scale, rather than in the retail department of England and the temperate zones generally. When the sun lifts his head above the horizon, you feel his force immediately, and have to guard yourself against his fierce heat; for nearly all the cases of sunstroke that I have known have been received before 7 a.m. When the winds blow, you are fully aware of the fact from the clouds of dust they raise, and from the rattling of the doors and windows. When it rains there is seldom any necessity to ask whether the clouds are pouring out their treasures, for it is almost literally true there "that it never rains but it pours." And in like manner when we think of the insect and reptile pests, we find that nature is most prolific.

In reading this chapter, I wish particularly to say that it will convey quite a false impression if it leads any one to imagine that these small causes of annoyance are always present;—it is only as one sits down quietly to think of and mass them, that the amount appears so large. How often it happens when we hear a story of accident, or spiritual appearance, or in fact anything startling, at once by the law of association we are led to think of similar events in our own experience, or in the experience of our friends. Circumstances long forgotten rise up vividly to memory, and one might almost fancy from the stories that are told, that one's life had been full of these unusual events. But this is far from being the case; the events narrated have been spread over a long lifetime. So it is with the subject of this chapter. The annoyance was not perpetual, and some of them have probably never been felt by many who have lived for many years in India.

The first of the insect tribe that calls for notice is the flea. I am aware that these interesting creatures are not unknown in England, and that they are capable of taming and domestication, of being harnessed to carriages, &c. I was greatly interested in an English watering-place to see an enterprising trainer of fleas advertising for one that had escaped from its stable, with its gold collar round its neck. Possibly, having regained its freedom, it reverted to its original condition as a plague, rather than a servant of man. But though they are occasionally found in England, I think that for size and numbers India is far ahead. It is not that they are always present, but I am inclined to think there must be a swarming time with them, that they come and go in myriads "all of their own sweet will;" or if they are under control, it must be that of a leader who did not make himself conspicuous as in olden times the leaders of our armies were wont to do. It may be that having had dreadful casualties amongst their officers, on the Darwinian theory the royal or aristocratic members of the flea world have found the wisdom of appearing very much like the rank and file.

My first experience of the havoc that an army of these small pests can make on the human body, was when I entered an empty house. As soon as I set foot in the place I was immediately conscious of irritation all over my body, and looking on my white trousers saw forty or fifty as large and lively as could be wished. I need not say that I made my escape as quickly as possible; but it was some time before I regained anything like freedom from their vicious attack. Twice in a lengthy residence in Calcutta we were attacked. On each occasion it was a few days after new mats had been laid on the floors, and the house thoroughly cleaned, that they made their appearance. They came in myriads. For about a week or ten days one was constantly hunting them from body and clothes. I have seen twenty or thirty at a time on my trousers. We sprinkled the floors with carbolic acid, kerosine oil, and other beautifully scented disinfectants, in the hope that we might make it uncomfortable for them, but as far as I could see it afforded no real benefit. They retired as suddenly as they came, and I confess I was not sorry when they departed. I do not know that they are more common in Bengali houses than in the houses of Europeans. I ought, perhaps, to say that except on these occasions when they came in wholesale consignments, we scarcely saw one. Fortunately for us, they do not form a constant, but only an occasional annoyance.

Next to fleas come "Norfolk Howards," as I understand they are euphemistically called in England. These are very common indeed in Bengali houses, and in the godowns or out-offices of the servants, but not at all common in those of Europeans. Having no paper on the walls, there are few places in which they can hide. And as the mattresses (of course feather beds are unknown in India) are taken out to be aired two or three times a week, the place is much too lively for these slow and nasty creatures. But one is sometimes a little horrified to see two or three of them crawling about the spotlessly white garments of some Bengali gentleman who may be seated in one's study. After his departure a good search is made, lest perchance one or two may have availed themselves of his visit to make a change of domicile. But bad though the ordinary European Norfolk Howard may be, there is a species peculiar to India far worse. These are about four times the size of the ordinary insect, and are supplied with wings. In Calcutta itself they are not frequently found; in fact I lived there for years without seeing one, or even hearing of them. But once when preaching I smelt one near, and found it had settled on my head. It was almost impossible to go on talking. My first experience of them in any numbers was at a small travellers' bungalow at the foot of the Himālayahs. In India, as

A TRAVELLERS' BUNGALOW.

there are hotels only in the large cities, along the most frequented roads the Government erect small houses called Dāk Bungalows, in which there are generally a couple of bedrooms, and a couple of sitting-rooms. The furniture is not very grand, consisting of a table, chairs, and bedsteads. A servant is in attendance, ready to prepare a meal at the shortest notice. As the carriage in which the traveller is riding draws near the house, he sees the servant chasing a chicken—a shrill cry is heard, and he knows that a victim has been killed, which in about half an hour he will see hot upon his table. A small charge is made for the use of the house, and in some of them one can be very comfortable.

After a journey of nineteen hours in a carriage that had been dragged by galloping ponies over a rough road, our party reached this house tired and hungry. We ordered dinner, and were sitting down to our soup when we became conscious of a most unpleasant smell. One of our number, being an experienced traveller, knew what had befallen us. "Flying bugs!" he cried, and in a few moments the table swarmed with them. The lamp had guided the Philistines to their prey, and I confess they proved too sharp for us. We tried to eat a little soup, but it was impossible; hungry as we were, we cleared away from the table and went dinnerless to bed, glad to get safely within the musquito curtains we had fortunately brought with us. My next experience was at a station about thirty miles distant from Calcutta, where I was a visitor for a fortnight. For several evenings it was impossible to have any light in the dining-room during dinner. All the lights were burning brightly in the adjoining room, where plates and saucers of water were placed on the tables, which proved fatal to many of these abominable insects. We managed to eat our dinner in a dim light without any accident. Occasionally I have seen or smelt one at other times, but not more than this; and I can honestly say I have no wish for a further acquaintance with them.

Next may be mentioned the plague of flies. In the hot and rainy seasons we have these in immense numbers, some small, some fine and large. But as flies are sometimes troublesome in England, I have only to say that if you multiply the greatest inconvenience from flies in England that you have ever known by about ten, you will know what India can do in this line. I remember conversing with a gentleman who did most splendid service in our army when for months they held the ridge from which the attack on Delhi was made during the mutiny of '57. He said during those months in tents there were many unpleasant things to bear, but *the* thing that he remembered most vividly as causing the intensest disgust was the plague of flies. As our army was in close quarters, they could not carry their offal very far away, so this must have attracted the flies from all parts of the country. The "Meat Market Review" of the fly world must have been widely circulated, and so they came in legions. It was with the greatest difficulty they could eat their meals without the addition of flies. The way that proved the greatest success was to hold a plate over the one on which the food was placed, and, watching their opportunity, to snatch a mouthful, and then let the plate fall over the food again.

Another pest, and a most destructive one to books and property, are the white ants. In the rainy season we see more of them than at other times, as they are driven from the ground by the rain and take shelter in the houses. It is because of the havoc caused by white ants that the beams of the houses in India are generally exposed; but so secretly do they work, that I have seen a beam of hard teak wood, 9 × 7 × 4, hanging together by a mere skin of paint, that it would have been almost possible to break it across one's knee, and yet to outward appearance the beam was solid as when new. They enter the part that is in the wall, and burrow to their hearts' content altogether unnoticed by those dwelling in the house. It is becoming more and more the fashion now to have iron beams in the houses. Books, too, they seem to be very fond of, and if a shelf has been undisturbed for a few weeks, it is not at all an uncommon experience to take down a book and find that it is half eaten—just a little powder being all that is left of a volume that contained the choicest thoughts of the greatest thinkers. Sometimes it seems as if they had a special fancy to the most costly books. A gentleman when coming home to England left his book-cases and books in charge of a friend; but as he had a few prizes and books specially valuable, he packed them in a tin-lined case, feeling sure that they would be secure. Judge of his vexation when the box was opened to find that they were completely ruined: not one remained uninjured. A small hole had been left in soldering the case, which the ants discovered, and whilst the owner of the books was enjoying himself in Europe, the ants held high festival in his case of books. Houses in India have to be repaired and thoroughly overhauled every four years. The plaster is chipped away, the ends of the beams and rafters exposed, and the woodwork all through the house most carefully examined, so that the doings of these workers in darkness may be fully revealed, and the losses made good.

I have reserved until last amongst the insects the musquito, because this is scarcely an intermittent pest but a permanent one. It is true that they are more numerous and vicious at some seasons than others, but I do not think we are ever absolutely free free from them. For my own part I must confess that, as a rule, they did not trouble me much. I have continued writing with half a dozen of them on my hand drinking their fill of my life-blood; but there was this grim satisfaction, that if they remained undisturbed and took as much as they could carry away with them, it would prove their death; and, further, if undisturbed, the after effect was less painful than if, being irritated, they left part of their boring apparatus in the skin. The only visible effects on my skin, if the part was not rubbed, was an almost invisible red speck. But to some people they are very troublesome. I have seen English people recently arrived in the country, who had not sought protection from these countless cormorants, and who could not bear the irritation caused by their bites without scratching them, look as if they were recovering from small-pox; and I have known some who for weeks could not wear stockings. Some people, though they remain many years in India, are almost as sensitive to a musquito bite as when they arrived: an immense blister rising where a really strong and vigorous insect had bitten them. But though some do not suffer much from the actual bite of a musquito, all suffer from the noise they make: it is like the war-shout of wild men playing upon the fears of a victim who sees no way of escape; or like the play of a cruel old cat with a mouse. If they would only bite and go, many people would not mind; but this constant buzzing noise, this perpetual sounding of the alarm preparatory to the attack, makes the most patient of mortals rather savage at times. At night, when within good net curtains that are fixed to the posts of the bed, one can lie and smile at their clarions; but if, alas, as often happens, the curtain has been torn, or carelessly tucked in under the mattress, woe betide you! for until the curtain is repaired, and the enemies that have gained entrance into the citadel expelled, there is no rest for you; for just as you are about to fall asleep the dreadful sound is heard, and you are very soon wide awake again. Some people find the nuisance so great that they have large curtains under which they place chair, table, and lamp, and thus are able to read and work in comfort. I should perhaps say that the musquito curtains are made more like a tent; *i.e.* there are four sides or walls, and a top the same size as the bed. These sides are tucked under the mattress, or, having shots at the bottom, fall on to the floor. In some houses, instead of the curtains being made the same size as the bed, a square frame is hung from the ceiling of the room, and a large net tent is suspended, which includes the bedstead, with a table and chair. Once within these curtains, if they be good, one can smile at the envenomed hosts outside shrieking in their fury. The Bengali name for these curtains is very suggestive; they are called Masāris, *i.e.* enemies of musquitos.

To give some idea of the numbers of these insects that infest an house, I may mention that one evening two ladies placed in heaps of a hundred the enemies they slaughtered. In about an hour they found they had each given a fatal blow to five hundred; they then gave up counting.

There is a fine kind of cockroach that is plentiful in India. They are about one and a half inches long, some even measuring two inches. These fly about, and at times hundreds of them may be seen if a box is left unmoved in a store-room for a few days. As long as they are content to remain in the store-room they do not cause much annoyance; but when they fly about the dining-room and settle on one's body during a meal, they become rather troublesome. The voyage out to India made us familiar with these things. The ship for some years had been running from London to Calcutta with a general cargo and passengers, from Calcutta to the West Indies with coolies, and from the West Indies to London with sugar. There had consequently been no really cold weather to destroy them, and whilst on board they had abundance of spoil. Their environment was most suitable, and they multiplied fast. The cabins swarmed with them, and as they seemed rather to like to feed on our nails, they managed to keep them short. I saw a bed in a lower cabin the counterpane of which was literally covered with them, so that it was impossible even to put the end of a pencil anywhere on the bed without touching them. Of course, the occupants who had paid for the cabin, after vainly trying to get rid of these interlopers, gave up in despair and slept in the saloon. Occasionally a cockroach was found in the puddings instead of a raisin: I need not say that after such a discovery plum-puddings were not very popular among the passengers.

Centipedes grow to a good size too, and in the rainy season are fairly plentiful. Though the small ones, those about a couple of inches long, are not attractive looking, nor are they nice to have on your body, they are greatly to be preferred to those that are about seven or eight inches long, and the width of one's finger. There is considerable strength, too, in their claws; they hold firmly where they seize. But fortunately we do not see a great number of these monsters. Hornets are pretty plentiful in some parts. One year, as there seemed to be an unusual number, and they were so vicious and spiteful that the servants could with difficulty cross the garden to the cook-room, we made a search, and found an immense nest about two feet long and one foot wide hanging from the bough of a tree. Had this been at a distance from the house I might have left it alone; but as the hornets became really dangerous to all who went near the bushes, as soon as it was dark we made torches of rag saturated with kerosine oil and gave them a happy despatch. In some districts in the rainy season small leeches abound. I was once walking with some friends, when, thinking that the perspiration was rather profuse, on looking at my legs I saw about half a dozen leeches hard at work filling themselves, and from two or three wounds the blood was oozing. I fancy that Indian leeches would be a capital investment, as in cases of blood-letting, if all are like those I saw, there would be no difficulty in getting them to bite.

In addition to those already mentioned, during the rainy season especially, a number of insects of all kinds crowd into the houses, so that around the lamps the tables are often well covered with those who have been drawn to their destruction by the glare of the light.

I shall now pass on to notice the larger orders of life. Amongst these the first that calls for notice are the frogs. People newly arrived from England are astonished at their very sad and painful cry. For months together, in the neighbourhood of a stream or tank, there seems to be an uninterrupted sitting of the Parliament of Frogs. Sometimes their conduct is quite orderly, one croaking at a time; at others it seems as if the whole house had risen, each one trying to outdo his rivals in noise. Unfortunately they do not remain in the gardens or fields, but come jumping about the house in goodly numbers, sometimes much to the terror of nervous and excitable inmates. In the dusk of the evening, as the doors and windows are wide open to admit as much air as possible, bats—rather large ones sometimes—come sweeping round, and every one is in mortal terror lest the poor misguided animals should settle on their heads. Towels are snatched up and there is a most exciting chase, which sometimes ends in the death of the bat, but far more generally in its escape into its own proper element—the darkness.

One of the commonest objects on the walls and ceilings of an Indian house are lizards of various sizes. These, by most people, are rather encouraged than otherwise, because they relish musquitos and flies as their most dainty food. Most exciting it is to watch them moving stealthily along, stalking a poor insect until near enough to make the final rush, and then to see their bright little eyes almost start from their head with excitement as they hurriedly eat their prey. They are very timid little creatures, though I have seen some so tame that they would come at the call of a whistle, and remain near enough to eat the flies that were given them. Although one likes to see the destruction of our natural enemies the musquitos, and feels indebted to the lizards for their kindness in freeing the houses from these pests, even a lizard is singularly out of place, and becomes an object of disgust, as it falls from the ceiling upon your naked body when entering your bath; especially if you are under the impression that it is a snake, who under such circumstances has a decided advantage over you.

From the lizard the transition to the alligators is most natural, seeing that they so much resemble them in appearance and in character. Many of the rivers in India abound in these frightful reptiles. I have often seen half a dozen lying together on the sandy bank of a river, basking in the sun. These reptiles are so quiet and stealthy, that unless great care is taken sometimes they will seize you as their prey. I have seen an alligator's head floating above the water, and had no idea that it was anything but a log of wood being carried down the stream; but as it neared the boat the head quietly sank under the water, and the animal moved away without so much as a ripple to mark his movement. Every year numbers of people are dragged under the water and go to provide nourishment for these repulsive creatures. I have heard of men sitting with a leg extending beyond the deck of their boat being seized; and of others being knocked out of the boat by the tail. Once caught by an alligator, there is not much chance for a man to escape. At the places where the villagers bathe, or fetch water, bamboo palisades are driven into the bed of the river, and thus leave a small space enclosed in which they are generally safe from attack. Sometimes the people attack them with spears and hatchets; but certainly in a fight the alligator has much the better chance of victory.

Now I come to the worst of all the pests of India—snakes. India is the home of many kinds of snakes, from the small and exceedingly pretty green snake, about three feet long and the size of the little finger, with bright red eyes, and not very poisonous; to the dreaded cobra or the monster python. Some people imagine that because snakes abound in India, that they are always to be seen. In the *city* of Calcutta I have not seen more than three or four; in the country districts I have seen perhaps twenty or thirty. Many English people have scarcely ever seen any. There is, however, this fear, that a snake *may* appear anywhere, and in many cases the bite of a snake means death within an hour. Often the pleasure one would have in visiting a ruin, or in walking through unfrequented woods, is marred by the thought that at any moment one may tread upon a snake and come to grief.

Although many thousands of people are said to die from the bite of snakes every year, it is noticeable that it is a most rare thing for a European to be bitten. I think this may be accounted for in two ways: Europeans wear boots which make a noise when walking, and the snakes hearing their approach escape—for if there is a possibility of getting away from man a snake will not attack; and secondly, the European wears clothes—if he be bitten the greater part of the poison would be absorbed by them, whilst in the case of a native the whole would be taken into the body. Some stories of narrow escapes might be told. A friend of mine seeing his wife about to go into the bedroom to fetch her bonnet, which she had worn only a few hours before, urged her to take a light. Fortunately for herself she did so, for coiled up in it was a large cobra. A story is told of an English nobleman travelling in India who, waking up, saw that a cobra had bitten his hand. With immense courage and great presence of mind he took up his revolver, blew off his hand, and saved his life.

I have heard from reliable eye-witnesses some wonderful stories of fights between snakes and other animals. A friend kept a black and tan terrier which was invaluable to him, as his house was frequently visited by snakes. This dog killed six large cobras. The same gentleman informed me that he once watched a most exciting fight between a goose and a cobra, in which the goose, after a struggle lasting twenty minutes, came off the victor. It ran round and round the snake until its opportunity came, and then rushing in, seized the snake by the neck and killed it. Monkeys are said to catch the snakes and grind the head on the ground until they come to the brain. The people believe that the monkeys know of some antidote for snake bite, for if ever they are bitten they rush off into the forests and re-appear after a time almost well.

Aliph Cheem, in a very interesting book called "Lays of Ind," gives a most amusing account of a bath-room adventure. Whilst a gentleman was bathing he heard the hiss of a snake, and saw the creature escaping by the drain. Wishing to have a little fun, when the snake was half through the hole he seized it by the tail, and after tugging away, at last pulled

AN UNPLEASANT VISITOR IN THE BATH-ROOM.

it out and flung it against the wall. To save himself from its attack he again jumped into his tub, and was surprised to see the cuteness of the snake; for this time, instead of going head first into the hole, it simply backed itself out through the drain, and with its distended hood effectually frightened away its tormentor.

VISHNU AND BRAHMĀ.

CHAPTER VI.

A CHAPTER ABOUT THE GODS.

To write a single chapter only about the many gods that are worshipped by the Hindus is not by any means an easy matter, as there are so many of them. If you ask a Hindu how many gods he worships, he will tell you at once that "there are 333,000,000!"

Now simply to write the names of this immense host would fill many chapters: but of course the people do not mean to say that they know the names of so many deities—it is simply a good round number which expresses the idea that they are more than can be reckoned. I shall try to give a brief account of those most generally known and commonly worshipped.

There is one thing very noticeable in the religious life of the Hindus, that though each person worships more particularly some one or more of the deities, they generally acknowledge the existence and power of them all. Many of the Brāhman worshippers of Vishnu, *e.g.*, to whom all life is most sacred, do not scruple to officiate as priests at the shrines of Kāli or Durgā, in whose worship goats and buffaloes are sacrificed. At their own private worship, after making an offering to their own special god, they throw a handful or two of rice, &c., on the ground as a gift to all the others, leaving each to take his proper share. And the ordinary people when visiting a holy place where they find a number of rival idols set up for worship, with their loud-voiced priests calling upon all to bring their gifts, after making an offering to the god that is specially worshipped there, do not fail to give something to each of the others, as they are in mortal terror lest by slighting one they bring upon themselves his anger, and be made to suffer for their neglect in this world or the next.

The belief that leads to the bestowal of gifts to the gods is this: that these beings, though living in their own proper heavens, far away amid the heights of the Himālayah Mountains, still have need of the food, &c., that earth produces, and that, in some mysterious way, the spiritual part of their gifts finds its way to the deities and supports them. In some temples silver chains are shown by which, it is said, the gods have been bound, until gifts flowed into the temple treasuries, which were spent in paying off the debts of these heavenly rulers. At other times, as will be seen later on, the gods are said to have resorted to real dishonesty in order to obtain the gifts of the people, which seem to be necessary to their well-being in heaven.

I. *Brahma.*

In speaking of the gods of India, first of all a word must be said about Brahma, the Supreme Being. He is declared to be without beginning or end, able to know all things, all powerful, and everywhere present, truthful, righteous, and pure. He is further described as being without form or shape. There are many amongst the more thoughtful of the people who declare that this is *the* object of their worship, although they take part in the worship of some of the many forms in which this Supreme Deity is said to have appeared on earth, beings who are said to have taught and done many things entirely contrary to his attributes as given above. It certainly does seem strange to see a man who declares that God is pure, prostrate himself before the image of Vishnu, who, according to their own sacred writings, in some of his incarnations, spoke what was false, and lived a life of impurity.

Brahma is the name under which God is known and worshipped by the new sects that have arisen within the present century, of whom Babu Keshub Chandra Sen was the most revered leader. This gentleman has rendered India an immense service in leading the better educated to regard the life and teaching of Jesus Christ with profound reverence. The members of these sects, many of whom have entirely discontinued the use of idolatrous rites and ceremonies, call their societies or churches Brahmo Somājes—*i.e.* Divine Assemblies, and in many respects approach in religious belief and practices to the Unitarians of Europe.

But it must be said that to the mass of the people Brahma, the Supreme Deity, is a name, and little more: he being quite eclipsed by some of the many forms that are declared to be his manifestations. Now-a-days it is most common for the Hindus to declare that, however different in character and conduct these incarnations of the Deity may be—although the teaching of some is in direct contradiction to that of others, nevertheless they are all forms of the One God. Formerly this was not by any means the case. The followers of one deity fought against the worshippers of others, and persecution has frequently been resorted to by those in power. The disciples of Buddha, who is said to have been an incarnation of Vishnu, were so ruthlessly persecuted, that all were either slain, exiled, or made to change their faith. There is scarcely a case on record where a religious persecution was so successfully carried out as that by which Buddhism was driven out of India. To-day the toleration is so great, that the Hindus frequently declare that though Hinduism is the best for Hindus, Christianity is the best for Christians, and Mahomedanism for the Mahomedans. It is only when an attempt is made to lead a man to change his religion that objection is raised against Christianity.

We now pass on to the chief manifestations of Brahma. These are three in number, which are commonly spoken of as the Hindu Triad, viz., Brahmā * the Creator, Vishnu the Preserver, and Siva the Destroyer. These three form what I believe were

BRAHMĀ.

once the only recognized incarnations of Deity; but in process of time other beings were deified, and, in order to obtain the reverence of the people, were declared to be further incarnations of Vishnu, the second person of the Triad—*i.e.* an incarnation of an incarnation of God. It was most natural that these

* Notice that the final ā in this the first person of the Triad is long; in the name of the Supreme Being it is short.

should be connected with Vishnu rather than Brahmā or Siva, because as *Preserver* it is to him that the gods or men resort for help in their difficulties. Each of these beings has a wife, who in some cases is more popular than her husband, and receives a far larger share of the gifts of the people.

In order to bring the connection between the deities distinctly to view, we will represent them in a small table.

BRAHMA (The Supreme).

Brahmā the Creator, and Sarasvati his wife.	Vishnu the Preserver, and Lakshmi his wife.	Siva the Destroyer, and Umā his wife.

1. *Brahmā the Creator, and Sarasvati.*

Brahmā is represented in images and pictures as a red man with four arms and four heads. It is taught that though originally he had five heads, he was deprived of one in an assembly of the gods and sages. A dispute having arisen between the three gods as to who was the greatest, each asserted his own superiority. Siva becoming angry as the discussion went on, caused his anger to assume a terrific form, which cut off the fifth head of Brahmā. From that time the Creator has had but four, and Siva is spoken of as Mahādeva or the Great God.

The worship of Brahmā has almost entirely ceased in India, so that there is but one temple existing in which offerings are made to him. When the Brāhmans in their daily devotions adore the sun, it is understood that some part of their worship is his share; but with this exception he is ignored. Two reasons are assigned for this. One of the sacred books teaches that because he had been guilty of gross sin it was decreed by the gods that in after times his worship should cease; but the people give a practical reason, as they say, "Since the work of the Creator is complete, no benefit can be gained by making offerings to him." In this sentence is given the key to the devotion of the Hindus: they bestow their gifts in the expectation that they will receive from the gods greater gifts in return; or they hope by their offerings to save themselves from their anger.

Of Sarasvati, the wife of Brahmā, there is not much to be said. She is styled the "Goddess of Wisdom," and is especially worshipped by those who, at school or college, wish to obtain her help for their work. An image of her is made and worshipped once a year. She is represented as a white woman with four arms, seated on a lotus, and is regarded as the inventor of letters and the founder of science. In some of the scriptures she is said to have forsaken her husband because he had taken another wife in her place, and in her anger to have pronounced curses on the other gods because they had recognized her rival; but according to one account she relented towards her husband and her rival, as "a wife ought to obey the wishes and orders of her husband, for the wife who reproaches her husband, and, instead of being his life, deprives him by her conduct of length of days, shall most assuredly go to hell."

II. *Vishnu the Preserver, and Lakshmi.*

This deity figures more largely in the Hindu scriptures, and attracts on the whole as much as, if not more worship than any of the others. When distress arose in heaven amongst the gods, or on earth amongst men, it was to Vishnu that resort was made, and by his help deliverance brought. Strange to say, the scriptures teach that it was because Vishnu, in order to enable the gods to overcome the demons in a great struggle, slew a woman, that the curse was pronounced upon him that he should be born into the world seven times. This was, however, modified; for as a curse once uttered cannot be recalled, it was declared that on each occasion these earthly lives should secure some benefit to mankind.

Vishnu is generally represented as a black man with four arms. It will be noticed that most of the gods have more than an ordinary supply of arms and eyes, the idea being to represent them as possessing more than ordinary wisdom and power.

Vishnu is worshipped by the more intelligent of the people as a spiritual Being rather than in any of the forms in which from time to time he appeared on earth. They regard him as the source of all things, the Supreme Deity. In their worship he is represented by an ammonite that is found in large numbers in Nipāl. These small fossils are regarded with the greatest reverence, and such was the superstition of my pundits, who were all worshippers of Vishnu, that I could never induce them to allow me to see their own, nor could I persuade them to obtain one for me. I have seen them only from a distance on shrines. The reason given for the ammonite being worshipped as Vishnu's representative is the following:—The deity seeing a lady named Tulsi, became devotedly attached to her. Lakshmi, the wife, being jealous, changed her into a plant, which bears her name. Vishnu at once assumed the form of this fossil shell that he might continue near his love. The plant is carefully tended by the Hindus, and the stone is treated as a human being, being carefully wrapped up in warm clothes in the cold season, and frequently bathed to keep it cool when the weather is warm.

Before speaking of the Incarnations of Vishnu, a word must be said about Lakshmi, his wife. The story of her appearance, which is very beautiful, will be given when describing the incarnations of Vishnu. She is regarded as the Goddess of Prosperity. To her the people look for long life, sons, riches, honours, and all the ordinary blessings of life. To say that she is a popular deity, is simply to say that in India as elsewhere people wish to be happy. In Britain, according to Carlyle, the most popular deity is "The God of Getting On." India has preceded us in having a special object of worship as the giver of worldly good. On the eve of her worship she is supposed to pass over every dwelling-place, and the people sit up all night amusing themselves, under the impression that her blessing is given to those only who are awake to receive it. When a man is prosperous, it is said that Lakshmi has come to live with him; when in adversity, that Lakshmi has forsaken him. She is represented as a beautiful woman with a golden complexion. A couple of elephants are standing by her side pouring large vessels of water upon her for her bath. It should be noted that in most of Vishnu's appearances on earth Lakshmi came too, and under different names was associated with him as his wife. This goddess is interesting to us in England, as it is from her name, which is commonly pronounced "Lucky," that we obtain the words "luck" and "lucky."

We now come to speak of Vishnu's incarnations.

VISHNU AS A FISH.

Generally they are reckoned to be ten in number, nine of which have already appeared—the tenth has yet to come.

1. *The Fish.*

In this shape Vishnu came to earth in order to

save a remnant of mankind from a flood that came to destroy the race, the account of which is a highly poetical form of that we have in the Book of Genesis. One day as a holy man named Manu went to a river to bathe, taking up a little water in his hands to wash his mouth, he was startled to hear a tiny fish address to him the words, "Save me." The fish explained that in the river there were larger fish that might seize him as their prey; he therefore asked the sage to place him in a jar, and then in a tank until he grew sufficiently large to take care of himself, and explained that he was Vishnu, who had assumed this form in order that he might save Manu and his family from a flood that was soon coming to destroy all other living creatures. Acting upon the fish's advice, Manu put him in a jar; then, as he grew larger, into a tank; and then cast him into the river, and set about the building of an immense ship. When all was ready the flood came, and the fish also appeared; but whilst destruction fell upon others, he towed Manu and his friends in their vessel to a place of safety.

2. *The Tortoise Incarnation.*

This form was assumed for the benefit of the gods rather than men. Formerly the gods and demons (*i.e.* beings who once were gods, but who, owing to their sin, had fallen from their high estate) were constantly engaged in a struggle for supremacy, sometimes the gods, sometimes the demons being the victors. At length the gods were told that if they could obtain the Amrita, or water of life, they would become so strong that their enemies would be easily overcome. This water could only be obtained by a mighty process of churning the sea. A great mountain offered to be the churning-stick, and the king of snakes the churning-rope; but what could be found strong enough for a pivot on which this mighty mountain

VISHNU AS A TORTOISE.

could be made to move? In their difficulty Vishnu came to the rescue, and as a tortoise sank to the bottom of the sea. When all was ready, the gods seized the tail and the demons the head of the snake, and the mountain began to revolve. After several objects that figure largely in Hindu legends came forth, the goddess Lakshmi or Sri, a perfect Venus, appeared, and with her the physician of the gods, holding a golden cup of nectar in his hand. Lakshmi was at once chosen by Vishnu as his reward. Now arose a quarrel: the demons demanded a share of the water as they had done a good share of the work. Vishnu again proved a helper. Assuming for a moment the form of his lovely bride, he ran away to attract the demons; and whilst they were engaged in the chase of a phantom, the gods quaffed the water of life and thus became strong enough to master their hereditary foes.

3. *The Boar Incarnation.*

In this strange form Vishnu came to earth to recover the most sacred books—the Vedas—which had been lost in the flood. It is by the knowledge of these Vedas that man can attain to the highest blessedness of heaven. They are the especial property of the Brāhmans—they only are permitted to read, or hear them read; and as the knowledge they convey is necessary to the attainment of the highest good, it follows of course that in this life the low-caste people have no immediate hope of reaching it. They have, however, this consolation, that if in the lower castes they do their duty after living a great many times on earth, they may at length be born as Brāhmans, know the Vedas, and by this means, after thousands of years, reach heaven's greatest bliss.

4. *The Man-lion Incarnation.*

This is a most striking illustration of the mutual hostility of the gods, and, with such a story as this, it is astonishing how men can for a moment profess to believe these various deities to be but manifestations of the One: and further, it is illustrative of the teaching which leads the people to believe that

VISHNU AS A MAN-LION.

they must acknowledge all the many gods of the Pantheon.

There was a king of the demons named Hiranyakasipu, who had received as a boon from Brahmā, in return for his devotion, the promise that no animal should slay him, that he should die neither by night or day, in heaven or in earth, nor by fire, water, or sword. Protected by this vast shield, he attacked the gods in heaven, wresting their treasures from them and usurping their functions. At length, his rapacity becoming unbearable, they proceeded to Vishnu for help. It so happened that this disturber of the peace had a son named Prahlāda who was a most devout worshipper of Vishnu, and the earnestness of the lad's faith simply drove the father to distraction. He forbade the son to reverence this god, seeing that all the gods were now under his control. But though recourse was had to the severest measures to lead him to recant, the boy remained unmoved. At length the father, who had been told by his son that Vishnu was everywhere present as the protector of his followers, striking a pillar, said, "Is he here?" He had no sooner spoken than the god appeared in the form of a being half man and half lion, and tore him to pieces. The promise of Brahmā had been kept in the letter though violated in the spirit. Vishnu came as no ordinary animal, and was neither man nor beast; he slew him in the evening, which is neither day nor night; the event happened under the eaves of the house, which place is said to be neither in heaven nor on earth; and he tore him to pieces with his hands, so that he was not injured by fire, water, or the sword. With such a story as this, it is not to be wondered at that the people should feel that it is not enough for them to be devoted in the worship of one only of the gods; they must try to be on good terms with all.

5. *The Dwarf Incarnation.*

This furnishes us with another most striking illustration of the duplicity that the gods have manifested, and which goes far to neutralize the beautiful passages

VISHNU AS THE DWARF, AFTER OBTAINING THE KING'S PROMISE.

which are to be found in the Hindu scriptures inculcating truthfulness. Actions speak louder than words; and with such conduct in the lives of their deities, it is not for a moment to be wondered at that the people should be untruthful and dishonest. So fully is this phase of the conduct of the gods understood, that it has passed into a proverb very widely known amongst the people, that "whilst the teaching of the gods is good and worthy of being heard, their conduct is bad and unworthy of imitation." This appearance of Vishnu upon earth was for the benefit of the gods rather than of man.

Bali, the grandson of Prahlāda, had by his great penance become so strong that he obtained supreme authority over the gods, who, being impoverished by this means, were in great distress. As usual they go to Vishnu, who promises to help them. With this object he comes to earth as a Brāhman dwarf, and presents himself in due course before Bali. As was customary, the king showed the greatest respect to his visitor, and at once asked what present would be acceptable to him. The dwarf appeared to be exceedingly modest, for he asked simply for as much land as he could step over in three strides. The king was amazed at the modesty of the Brāhman, and at once granted his request; but bitterly did he regret his bargain. No sooner were the words spoken than the dwarf began to grow, and his height became such that with two steps he stepped over the universe, and then had no place for his foot to rest upon. Fearful at having broken his promise, the king lays down his head for his visitor to place his foot upon it, saying that he feared hell itself less than a bad name. Upon this he was sent to hell because he had not kept his word to a Brāhman. The other gods seemed to have had a little more conscience than Vishnu; they thought it was rather too bad to take all that the king had and then to punish him in addition, so they asked their great helper to remit the latter part of the sentence, to which a partial consent was given.

6. *The Parusarāma Incarnation.*

The name Vishnu bore at this visit to the earth means "Rāma with the axe," and is to distinguish him from the far more important incarnation as Rāma Chandra. There were evidently fierce and protracted struggles for supremacy between the Brāhmans and the next great caste, the Kshatriyas or Warriors. It was the duty of the members of the warrior caste to rule, to wage war, to protect the country; but it was equally their duty to have Brāhman counsellors—in other words, to rule the world for the advantage of the priests. They did this for a time, but evidently some turbulent spirits arose who were not so obedient to priestly rule, and attempts were made to free themselves from the yoke. But in the long run the Brāhmans gained the victory, for it is asserted that Vishnu came in this form, and not once only but on several occasions utterly destroyed the race, excepting a few who hid themselves from their destroyer. The fact remains that whilst the Brāhmans are everywhere to be found in India, in many places with but slightly diminished power, the Kshatriyas are very few in number and are found only in a very few districts.

7. *The Rāma Chandra Incarnation.*

This is one of the most beautiful and interesting of all the Hindu legends. The story is told at great length and with great beauty in the Rāmāyana, one of the two great epic poems of India.

As Vishnu came in the form of the man-lion to destroy

Hiranyakasipu, and as the dwarf to wrest his kingdom from Bali, as Rāma Chandra he came to destroy the same being now known on earth as Rāvana, the hundred-handed demon who ruled in Ceylon. As the destroyer was the same, so the object of his anger was the same, who, after suffering in hell the penalty of his crimes, appeared again on earth. The Hindus do not believe in annihilation. Gods die and live again, so do men and demons.

When Vishnu appeared in the form of Rāma, he came of a princely family. There were, however, three wives in the home and four sons; but although Rāma was the heir-apparent, in order that there might be peace in the palace, he left home and country, and, with his lovely wife, Sitā, took up his abode as a hermit in a forest. It was a common experience for men in those times to forsake the cities for the quietness and repose of the woods. One day as he was absent from the hermitage Rāvana appeared, seized Sitā, and carried her off in a most wonderful aerial car to his home in Ceylon. On his return, unable to see his wife, Rāma was overwhelmed with grief. He had no idea where she had gone until a large crane, which had been mortally wounded fighting in her defence, told him who was the thief.

But now a difficulty arose as to her present abode. In his distress he applied to the king of the monkeys, as the aboriginal inhabitants of India are styled in the Hindu books, by whose aid an immense army of monkeys was raised, amongst whom Hanumān was most conspicuous in his friendship for Rāma and in the service that he rendered. It is owing to this story that monkeys are now worshipped in India.

After a lengthened search, Hanumān found her in Ceylon, and managed to convey to her the assurance that her deliverance would be effected. As there was no means of communication between the mainland and the island, it is said that the monkeys constructed a bridge, over which the army of rescue marched,

HANUMĀN, THE MONKEY GOD.

and, after a tremendous war, Rāma succeeded in slaying Rāvana, and in rescuing his wife.

This book is most interesting to Europeans, but the fascination it has for the Hindu, who receives all its wonderful stories as truth, is marvellous. This incarnation has supplied millions with an object of worship, and it is the name of Rāma that is repeated in their hearing as they die, and that is recited as their dead bodies are being carried to the riverside to be burned. Often have I heard the mourners go by my house repeating, in a monotonous chant, "Rāma, Rāma, Satya Nāma," *i.e.* "Rāma, Rāma, the true name." This, I think, is because of the statement that when Rāma's monkey auxiliaries had nearly all been slain in his behalf, he cried to Yama, the god of the spirit world, who at his request released them from his kingdom, and permitted them to return to carry on their leader's war to a successful issue.

8. *Krishna and Balarāma.*

These two together form the eighth incarnation in those books which reckon Buddha as the ninth; but when Buddha is left out of the list, Krishna is the eighth and Balarāma the ninth. Of Balarāma there is nothing special to say, except that he was the faithful friend and companion of Krishna.

The fullest account of Krishna is in the Vishnu Purāna, a book that most probably was not written earlier than the eighth century A.D., evidently by one who had some acquaintance with the New Testament. It is very interesting to see how in Krishna's life several events in Jesus' life have been borrowed; or, to say the least, the coincidences are such as to lead to the conclusion that the one book largely influenced the writer of the other. The Hindus see this distinctly, and some of them affirm that the life of Jesus was written under the influence of the life of Krishna. Unfortunately for this view of the case, the Hindu book is nearly seven hundred years later than the New Testament.

The names are exceedingly alike in sound—Kreeshta

and Kreesht, — as they are pronounced in India. As Herod, fearing that a child born in Bethlehem was to become King of Israel, ordered the slaughter of the children of that village, so Kansa, king of Mathura, being told that the son of certain

KRISHNA.

parents would prove dangerous to him, ordered a similar destruction of infants; but the one he wished to be rid of was miraculously saved. This Kansa, it should be mentioned, was none other than Hiranyakasipu, Bali, and Rāvana, who in previous incarnations had fallen victims of Vishnu's power.

Miracles are not commonly ascribed to the Hindu deities, but Krishna is reported to have performed many, some of them bearing a striking likeness to those of the New Testament. On one occasion, when walking through a street, a poor deformed flower-girl presented him with a flower. This so delighted the young deity that he touched her and made her whole. The cowherds amongst whom he lived, being worshippers of Indra, the ruler of the firmament, determined that as they had a god living amongst them they would present their gifts to him rather than to Indra. The king of heaven, incensed at this slight, sent a tremendous storm to destroy them; whereupon Krishna took up a mountain upon his finger, which he held as a gigantic umbrella over the land, and protected them against the anger of their offended deity. As Jesus prayed for His murderers, "Father, forgive them, for they know not what they do," as it was "through ignorance" that the Saviour of men was slain, so was it with the death of Krishna. When an old man, as he was walking in a wood, a huntsman, mistaking him for a stag, shot an arrow which pierced his heart, and thus ignorantly caused his death.

The character of the two, however, has no similar features. Whilst Jesus' life, the more it is studied, the more beautiful and divine does it appear; the character of Krishna from childhood to age was morally bad. As a child he manifested superhuman skill and power, which he employed in gratifying his own wishes. As a man he was the incarnation of impurity: he himself refusing to retain possession of a certain gem which had the power of working ill for its possessor who did not live a good life. He did not scruple to steal what he could not get by lawful means, and his followers—and they are very numerous—are amongst the most immoral of all the Hindus. This is not at all surprising when it is known that although his wife Lakshmi had been born into the world as his companion in this incarnation as in his previous ones, she is not the woman who is always associated with him in worship, but Rādhā, the wife of a cowherd. As one walks through the streets, it is no uncommon thing to hear a man repeating the name of this deity as part of his religious exercises; but invariably Rādhā's name is associated with that of Krishna—"Rādhā Krishna, Rādhā Krishna," being the formula repeated hundreds of times.

Krishna accomplished the purpose of his mission to earth at a grand tournament. Kansa, having heard of his prowess, made great preparations for a tournament, to which he invited the strongest wrestlers and the bravest warriors in his kingdom. His orders were for Krishna to be slain by fair means or foul. After the hero had destroyed several of these hired assassins, he made a rush at Kansa and put an end to him.

There is one special feature in the worship of Krishna that calls for notice; it is that songs have been written in which the most passionate love for the deity is expressed, the singing of which forms an important part in all his festivals. Of the other deities the people stand in the greatest fear, and when they approach a temple, go with trembling, lest inadvertently they should offend the deity represented, and bring upon themselves his anger. But Krishna seems to be regarded somewhat differently, though it must be stated that it is not pure love for man that is celebrated in their songs. It is a singular fact that at the time Luther was preaching so powerfully the doctrine of salvation by faith in Jesus Christ throughout Europe, a great reformer in Bengal was preaching salvation by faith in Krishna; and although he taught his disciples to do many things that were contrary to the ordinary teachings of Hinduism, it is estimated that about one-sixth of the Hindus in Bengal are his followers to-day. At the Krishna festivals there is far more of gladness and pleasure than at any of the others.

9. *Buddha.*

In some though not in all the lists of Vishnu's appearances on earth, Buddha appears as the ninth. In this more than in anything I know, the cleverness of the leaders of Hinduism is to be seen. Gautama, the Buddha,* or the Enlightened One, rose as a reformer, a teacher of doctrines quite opposed to the Hinduism of the past. He gave up home, a palace, a crown, a wife, that he might discover and then teach men how to live so as to avoid the ills of life. And when he had tried every form of Hinduism and found them wanting, he arranged his own teaching, and by the earnestness of his life and the beauty of his character attracted followers, who, fired with his enthusiasm, strove to establish his religion. Such was their earnestness and zeal, that in a few centuries, in a large part of India, Buddhism took the place of Hinduism. After a

* Sākya was the name of his family, Gautama of his tribe; Buddha is an appellation meaning the Enlightened One, just as Christ means the Anointed.

time Buddhism in its turn grew feeble; and after a most fierce struggle Hinduism, in a changed form, utterly annihilated Buddhism. Its monasteries and temples were razed to the ground, its priests and people either slain, exiled, or brought over to the new form of faith.

Now power so great as that which Gautama had manifested, the leaders of Hinduism saw could not be ignored. What more natural, then, than to regard him as Vishnu in another form? But he led the Hindus away from Hinduism! Could a god do that? Yes! say these teachers, if it is for a good purpose. And so the following account of the transaction is given:—There was a dreadful famine, and Brahmā told a certain prince that as he was the only righteous man, if he would reign over the earth, the gods would serve him and men would be happy. To this the prince consented on one condition—that the gods forsook the earth, and allowed him to have undisputed sway. This was agreed to, and the prince, taking the name of Dīvodāsa (the servant of the gods), set up his throne at Benares, and for eight thousand years the people were supremely happy. Not so, however, the gods. They wished to visit their old places of resort on earth to receive the gifts and adoration of the people. How could this be obtained? As long as the people were good and Dīvodāsa reigned justly, the arrangement could not be altered. Vishnu then suggested that he should come on earth as a new teacher, lead men into error, that there might be a sufficient reason for the interference of the gods. He came in the form of Gautama, and his wife as a female devotee, and they succeeded so well in their false teaching that men fell into sinful paths, and the gods regained their position on earth. It is dreadful to imagine how men could have sunk so low as to teach and receive such a story as this ; that a god could come to earth to lead men from virtue to vice, from truth to falsehood.

10. *The Kalki Incarnation.*

This appearance has yet to be accomplished—Vishnu has yet to come to inaugurate a kingdom of universal righteousness, peace, and prosperity. Reading the accounts in the Hindu scriptures, and comparing them with the Book of the Revelation, no impartial person can hesitate for a moment to see that this idea has been borrowed entirely from St. John's book. This king is to ride upon a white horse, and under his rule universal happiness is to be enjoyed.

III. *Siva, the Destroyer.*

We now come to the third person of the Hindu Triad, Siva, or, as he is far more commonly called, Mahādeva, the great god.

This deity is not said to have come in various forms to earth, but rather to have dwelt there regularly, chiefly at Benares the sacred city of the Hindus, having his heaven amid the inaccessible peaks of the Himālayahs. Why he should be called the Destroyer, it is not easy to see, as the word really means, "The Bright or Happy One." The only reasonable suggestion I can offer is, that as there was a Creator, and a Preserver, a Destroyer was wanted to complete the system. Certainly he has nothing to do with death, or with the regions of the dead.

Siva is usually painted as an almost naked man,

having his body covered with ashes, and a tiger-skin wrapped round his loins. Around his neck and in his matted hair are cobras, the most deadly snakes in India. He usually has a sort of lute in his hand, whilst

SIVA.

his eyes and general appearance indicate a person in a state of intoxication. This appearance is in harmony with his character and conduct as described in the Hindu scriptures. He is said to have spent his time in begging, and was addicted to the use of spirits and bhang, a strong intoxicant made from hemp. The account of his life occupies a large space in the books, but I do not remember one good thing that he is said to have done. And yet the worship of Siva is perhaps more widely spread than that of any of the Hindu deities. In the temples it is not usual for him to be represented by an image, but by an upright pillar of stone, to which the greatest reverence is paid by all classes of the people.

Siva is, however, quite eclipsed in the popular mind of Bengal by his wife, who at different times has re-appeared on earth, and by some means or other regained her husband's affections. The fact that she has pronounced most dreadful curses on any who worship her whilst neglecting her lord, may to some extent account for the more common worship of Siva. I will give a very brief account of three of the forms under which she is known:—

1. As Parvati, in the earlier ages of Hinduism, she was the faithful wife of Siva, who even then is said to have lived the same disreputable life as in later years. Because of the misconduct of her husband, her father refused to invite him to a great sacrifice he was celebrating. Parvati was so incensed at this, that she threw herself into a fire and was burned to death. For this reason she is sometimes called Sati, the faithful one, and has given a name to those widows who, when their husband's body was being burned, chose to be burned alive with it.

2. As Durgā she slew a great giant or demon named Durga, when she appeared on earth to destroy immense numbers of these beings. The accounts of the war, which continued for a long time, are very

voluminous, and the tales of Jack the Giant Killer are tame in comparison with the deeds of prowess of this deity. The festivals of the Durgā Puja are the most popular of all in Bengal; business being almost entirely suspended for twelve days. She is represented in idols as a most beautiful and attractive woman, with ten arms, and a most calm and benignant face.

DURGĀ.

3. As Kāli she is, as the name implies, black in colour, and certainly anything more frightful than her face it would be hard to imagine; but a more detailed account of her will appear in a description of her temple.

Ganesa, the God of Wisdom, is regarded as the son of Siva and Durgā, when in an earlier life she was known as Parvati. Ganesa is rather the god of cunning than of wisdom. An image or picture of him is seen in most places of business, and as soon as the office or shop is opened, the owner bows down to Ganesa as the one who will enable him to do well in his business.

This god has an elephant's head, which he obtained in a strange way. The sun called to offer his congratulations to Parvati when her son was born. She, fearing that his beams might injure her child, asked him not to look at him; but this warning being disregarded, his rays burned the child's head. The mother asked her husband to provide another head for the babe. He

GANESA, THE GOD OF WISDOM.

seeing an animal, but being in a state of intoxication not noticing that it was an elephant, cut off its head and placed it upon the child's body, and so Ganesa has always carried the mark of his father's intemperance.

CHAPTER VII.

HINDU TEMPLES.

THE temples of the Hindus being built to serve a very different purpose from that for which Christian churches are erected, it is only natural that they should be of a very different style. Christian churches are built in order that a congregation may unite in the worship of God; and are arranged so that all may hear the Scriptures read, join in praise and prayer, and listen to the instructions in religious doctrines and exhortations to faith and holiness that the minister has to deliver. The Hindu temples have no accommodation for a worshipping assembly, the great majority of them being only just large enough for the image they shelter and the priest to officiate at the altar. Even the larger temples have no seats, nor does a congregation stand long in front of the shrine: the people simply bow to the image, give their offerings to the priest, and move away.

Most of the temples have been built by individuals who wished by this means to provide an atonement for sins committed. According to the teaching of Hinduism, to each act of a man's life a certain reward or punishment is attached, which must be enjoyed or endured in this world or the next. Having no knowledge of the infinite love of God, and knowing nothing of the Saviour's great work, the Hindu wishes to get

GROUP OF HINDU TEMPLES.

deliverance from the punishment of his sins, and to rise from his present position, that when next he appears on earth he may be born in a Brāhman's family; because every one must live on earth many times as Brāhmans before they can return to God from whom they came, and be saved from the necessity of being born again into the world. Their scriptures teach that certain acts will not only free a man from the penalties of sin and give him a certain amount of happiness in heaven, but also secure the still greater good of causing him in his next earthly life, if not to be born as a Brāhman, yet to rise a step higher in the ladder, and bring him a little nearer to that position in which he may hope for the greatest bliss of heaven, viz., absorption, or return to the Ocean of Deity. Building a temple is one of the many "works of merit" which will have this great influence on a man's future. As, therefore, the building of a temple is productive of such great benefit, to build seven temples, or thirteen, or twenty-one, will naturally be still more productive of good. No instruction being given respecting the size a temple should be, the people, anxious to profit by this means, build them as small as they possibly can, and prefer to spend £1000 in building seven or more, rather than the same amount upon one. This is not the universal rule; but it accounts for the fact that often where one only is necessary there are seven or thirteen, *one* of them only being used, the others remaining closed. And, as a further effect of the same cause, new temples rise whilst close beside them old ones are allowed to fall into ruin. The man who built them it is believed is now reaping the reward of their erection; were another to spend money on their repair, the merit would go to the original builder rather than to the restorer. Hence we find that many beautiful temples are allowed to crumble into ruin, because it is not to the interest of men now living to spend money upon them.

KĀLI DANCING ON HER HUSBAND, SIVA.

Most of the temples are not larger than about eight or ten feet square. The image occupies perhaps two feet of this; the space in front being for the priest as he mutters the texts, rings his bell, and offers fruit, flowers, leaves, and water to the idol. The people do not enter the temple, but stand outside whilst the priest presents their gifts, as they are not allowed to offer anything direct; all they give, with an accompanying fee, must be handed to the priest of the temple, who lays it before the image. Even in the houses where idols are set up for worship, the ordinary Hindu cannot officiate before it; he must engage a priest to perform the religious rites on his behalf. In the larger temples, when the pilgrims draw near to the idol, they ring a bell in order to attract his attention. As the suppliants approach the image, they are filled with fear lest they should inadvertently awaken the anger of the deity they have come to worship.

I will now give some account of the large temple at Kāli Ghāt, near Calcutta; a holy place to which the people come from all parts of India because of the great benefits a visit is supposed to give.

When this temple was originally built it is not easy to say; a remote antiquity is given to it by the following legend. When Siva saw his wife destroy herself in the fire because of the slight her father had shown to her husband, being distracted with grief, he took up her dead body, and wandered from place to place with it across his shoulder. Wherever he came, sickness and all kinds of evil followed. The inhabitants of the world, in their distress, appealed to Vishnu, who had a marvellous quoit, with which he performed great marvels. This he threw with such force, that it cut up the body of the goddess into fifty pieces. Wherever a part of this body fell, a temple rose. It is said that at Kāli Ghāt there is the second toe of her left foot. I have, of course, never seen this relic, nor have I seen any one who has done so; but in the belief of the people it is there.

The temple is an immense source of profit to its owners, as they receive about 7½d. as a fee from every goat that is sacrificed there. The priests and all the numerous attendants are in the service of the family that profits by the devotion of the numerous pilgrims.

The temple stands on the banks of a small stream that is believed to have once been the bed of the Ganges. It is almost hidden by a number of small shops, as the pilgrims who visit this holy place are anxious to take home mementos of their visit and presents for their friends. In front of the temple proper is a platform with a roof, but no walls, where a number of Brāhmans are always to be seen reading the sacred books or repeating the names of the gods. In front of this platform are the frames fixed in the ground for holding the victims that are there to be sacrificed. On the other side of the platform is the shrine, between which and the platform is a narrow passage, by which the visitors pass in front of the image.

The shrine contains the image of Kāli—a most repulsive-looking object. She is represented as a black woman, with three glaring eyes, the third being in her forehead. Her huge tongue, made of bright gold, protrudes from her mouth, reaches to her waist, and is seen better than any other part of the image. For earrings she has two human heads, a garland of human skulls for a necklace, and a waistband formed of human hands. All these decorations she is supposed to have taken from the enemies she slew during her visit to the earth. She stands on the body of her husband.

The explanation of this attitude is as follows: When she had completed the destruction of her enemies she began to dance with joy. This dancing was so violent that the earth trembled, and it seemed probable that it must be shaken to pieces. In their distress the people cried to her husband for help, but at first he thought it useless to interfere. As, however, the people clamoured for his protection, he lay on the ground amongst the dead bodies of his wife's foes. Looking down, and seeing her husband under her feet, she became overcome with shame, and put out her tongue, which is the way in which Bengalis blush to this day, and at once desisted from her violent dancing.

The reason assigned for offering the blood of goats and buffaloes to Kāli is one connected with her wars. On one occasion, when faint with her destructive work, she wanted some refreshment. Seeing nothing else at hand, she quaffed the blood of her enemies. Formerly the people offered human sacrifices to her, but as this cannot now be done, goats and buffaloes are slain, in the belief that, seeing the blood, the deity will remember her pleasure in drinking the blood of her enemies, and, being pleased, will listen graciously to the prayer of the suppliant. At certain times the number of victims slain in front of this image is so many, that the courtyard streams with blood, and the stench is really sickening.

It must not be supposed that people come regularly to this temple as we are in the habit of attending church on Sundays. There are certain days of the year, it is true, when year after year people go there, in the hope of obtaining her protection for the coming months; but generally speaking it is on special occasions, either to ask for some particular gift, or to return thanks for some specific blessing. Frequently it is for sons, or for wealth, that the people visit Kāli Ghāt. A family is engaged in a lawsuit. As the case is coming on, the head and other members of the family set off to the temple, and there offer a goat, in the hope that this will cause the goddess to take an interest in them, and cause them to succeed. But far more frequently it is in connection with family matters. I will give a typical case.

A husband and wife had lived together for years, but no son was born. This was to them a most dreadful evil. The husband knew that if he died without a son there was no one who would properly perform his funeral rites for years after his death, and believed that in consequence of this his spirit might wander in misery, unable to gain admission to heaven. The wife knew that unless she had a son her husband might bring home a second wife, and her position in the home be given up to her rival. There was the truest love between the two, and many an hour's misery and anxiety they experienced because there was no son to gladden the home. At last, in a solemn hour, husband and wife cried to Kāli, and said, "O Kāli Mother, we are childless; have pity on us! Give us a son to love, and to be our support in this life, and our saviour from ills in the next. We promise that if thou art gracious we will go on a pilgrimage to thy shrine, and there sacrifice a goat for thy pleasure. Hear and answer us quickly, O Kāli." In due time a son was born, and the joy of their hearts was boundless. But although pleased with the little babe, they did not at once rush off to the temple to fulfil their vow; it was not until the child was about seven years of age that the journey was undertaken. The parents wished to be quite sure that he would live before they incurred the expense and fatigue of such a journey. At last, on a favourable day, father, mother, and son went to the temple, sacrificed the goat, and fulfilled their promise. Hanging from the trees near the great temple numberless little stones or lumps of mud are to be seen; these are pledges of anxious, sorrowing pilgrims who have come there to ask for some blessing. These worthless reminders are left there until the prayer is answered; and when the thing asked for is granted, the people come again with the gift they had pledged themselves to give. It is most touching to see the earnestness and almost despairing look of many as they approach the temple, and one's heart goes out in sympathy with them, as one cannot but pray that they may quickly know that their great Father in heaven is waiting to bless; more ready to give good gifts to all his children than they are to ask them at his hands.

On the days specially sacred to Kāli in some one or other of her forms, the Hindus flock in immense crowds to this temple. But the shouting, crowding, and gesticulating of the people, are utterly opposed to anything approaching a devotional spirit. The aim of each seems to be to hurry to the priest with his present, make his offering, and get away as quickly as possible. There is no prayer, no hymns of praise; just a scramble to get to the front of the image, and then a hasty return.

On certain days of the year that are sacred to her

husband, Siva, the crowds are not only large, but boisterous and noisy. Processions with music are formed, and men and boys march to her temple dressed and painted to represent the gods and demons. Many of these are completely intoxicated with hemp, and their words and acts most repulsive. They cut themselves with knives, and burn incense in small iron pans, which are attached to their bodies by iron handles; it is really more like the worship of demons than of God. The people believe that bodily pain and human blood are pleasing to Siva; hence the sufferings they inflict upon themselves in his worship.

It is interesting to know how the idols are treated that are set up in the temples. In a word, I may say that it is the duty of the priests to attend to them just as though they were alive. At sunrise, a bell is rung to awaken them from sleep. Before opening the door, the priest knocks for permission to enter. If the image is small and movable, it is then raised up from its bed; but if it is a fixture, it is taken for granted that it is now ready for its morning ablutions. First a little water is brought to wash its mouth; and then fruit is put before it to eat, and sherbet is given it for drink. Its clothes are chosen of various kinds for different seasons of the year: in the summer they are thin and cool, in winter warm and thick; and a punkah, or fan, is waved over its head in the hot weather to keep it cool. After breakfast it is supposed to be receiving visitors until about noon, when it is put down to sleep. After a couple of hours' rest it is again raised, and amusements, such as music and dancing, are provided for its entertainment. After the evening meal it is carefully laid down to rest, the lamps of the temple are extinguished, and the doors closed for the night. Just as a little girl plays with and speaks to her doll as though it were a living child; so the Hindu priests in the temples treat the images. Where the idols are too heavy to be moved, the same formalities are gone through, only in this case often a smaller idol is dressed as the representative of the larger one. And so superstitious are the people, that they would not dare to intrude upon the priest as he is engaged in these ceremonies.

In many of the villages where there is no temple, a shapeless stone, placed under a tree, is as carefully treated by its priest as the elaborately carved idol in a beautiful temple, and is as devoutly worshipped by the villagers.

The nearest approach to a Christian congregation amongst the Hindus is an assembly of people gathered together to hear a Kathak read the scriptures. Sometimes in a quiet place near a temple, sometimes under the shade of a tree, a man will be seen seated on a small platform with a great crowd, whose attention is most rapt, as he reads for hours together from some of their most sacred books. Rich men often seek by this means to gain merit in heaven, or remission of sins. Many of the Hindu scriptures distinctly promise heaven to those who read or hear these writings. When it is remembered that very few of the people can read, and that the sacred books which it is lawful for the people to hear are full of most pathetic and interesting stories, it is not to be wondered at that the people should flock in crowds to hear them, or that they should gladly give their attention to them for hours together.

CHAPTER VIII.

HOLY PLACES AND PILGRIMS.

HINDUISM is pre-eminently a religion of forms and ceremonies. It teaches the masses of the low-caste people that certain acts must be performed in order that prosperity may be enjoyed in this life and happiness secured in the next. And it is a noticeable fact that whatever may be the duty the writer of the scripture may be speaking of at the time, it is said to be *the* one that is supremely and indispensably necessary. At one time it is bathing, at another it is worshipping an idol, at another it is feeding the hungry, and at another it is visiting some of the many holy places. And although the distinct assurance is given that whoever performs the duty spoken of will attain the highest bliss possible for him, the mind is unable to obtain satisfaction because other teachers speak of other duties as equally necessary to salvation. The Hindus in the hands of their religious guides are in the condition of the old man who in the fable is represented as trying to please everybody; but who in the end pleased nobody, and lost his ass into the bargain.

Pre-eminent amongst their many religious duties is that of visiting some of the many holy places.

Some people start on a lengthened tour from shrine to shrine; but as this is a very costly affair owing to the presents they have to give to the guardians of the temples, in addition to the expenses of travelling, the mass of the people have to be content with visiting one of these places only. Yearly, thousands of

A BRÂHMAN WORSHIPPING THE GANGES.

poor men and women are to be seen trudging along to some distant temple or bathing-place, who have been anticipating this journey for many years and have denied themselves of almost the necessaries of life, in order that they might thus secure the favour of the gods: and I have never seen greater religious fervour anywhere than that which is depicted on the faces of those who for the first time come in sight of the holy place at Saugar Island, where the waters of the Ganges mingle with those of the sea, or of Benares, *the* sacred city of the Hindus. The people are very ignorant, very superstitious, but very earnest in their belief that good must come to them from a visit to these shrines.

A volume might be written on this subject with a description of the many "holy places" in India, each of which promises some particular good; I can only give a very brief account of four of the most noted and popular in Northern India. It should be noticed that these are highly esteemed, not only by the people in the neighbourhood: I have seen pilgrims who have come a thousand or fifteen hundred miles to obtain the blessing a visit is said to give.

1. *Ganga Sāgar.*

This shrine is on Saugar Island, at the mouth of the river Hugli. The great object of a visit here is, by bathing in the river, to obtain freedom from sin. Very explicit is the promise in the Rāmāyana, one of the most interesting of the Hindu sacred books—"Bathing in the Ganges will destroy all sins past, present, and future." But although the Ganges is fifteen hundred miles long, and the people who live near bathe in its waters every day, there is a general belief that once at least in a lifetime, they ought to bathe at this spot. Hence in January there are three specially holy days, during which as many as 100,000 people collect together at Saugar Island from all parts of the country. Many of the pilgrims are widows, and old people, who have most carefully put aside a trifle from their scanty earnings through many long years, in order to get rid of sin before they appear in the presence of Yama, the judge of the dead. The story that leads the people to bathe here is most interesting, and is a fair sample of the legends which awaken and sustain the faith of the people in their religious duties.

There was a king named Sāgar—from whom the island gets its name—who for many years after his marriage had no son. As was usual in such cases, he appealed to the gods. After weary years of waiting, the promise was given that he should have not one only, but 60,000. When this immense family had grown up, Sāgar wished to exchange his earthly throne for that of heaven. Mortals had frequently been promoted through their religious deeds to this position; Sāgar made the attempt. In order to obtain this boon, it was necessary to perform a great sacrifice in which a hundred horses were killed. Arrangements were made, the guests invited, and the ceremonies satisfactorily performed until the last day of the feast came. In order to the offering of a perfect sacrifice the last horse (one having been daily offered for ninety-nine days) must not be tied up in a stable during the night preceding the morning of its death, but be allowed to wander where it would. When, however, the morning dawned, it could not be found. Indra, the reigning king of heaven, had come down at night and stolen it, because he knew that if the sacrifice were completed, he would be compelled to resign his throne to Sāgar.

The loss of the horse caused the greatest trouble, as no other could be substituted for it. The princes wandered far, and after a long search found it tied to a tree on Saugar Island close beside a saint named Kapila, who was engrossed in religious meditation. When they saw the horse the princes, imagining Kapila to be the thief, poured forth their wrath upon him; and he in his turn, growing angry because his meditations had been disturbed, cursed them, and they became a heap of ashes. When the news reached the king his sorrow was unbounded. He resigned his throne and gave up his life to the performance of religious duties, with the object of gaining their restoration to life. At his death, a son who had been left at the palace, and so escaped the sad fate that befell his brothers, took up the work; but he, too, died without being able to accomplish it. His son, who in a similar manner devoted his life to the same object, was more successful. Being informed that if Ganga (the river Ganges), who as a goddess had hitherto lived in heaven, which is supposed to be in the inapproachable snows of the Himālayahs, would but come down and touch these ashes, the princes would regain their life, he entreated her with such persistency to grant him this favour, that she at last consented. In her fury at being disturbed, she first jumped upon Siva's (her husband) head, and was held in the coils of his hair until she grew calm, and thence sprang to the ground. From the foot of the mountains she marched to Saugar Island, and no sooner touched the ashes than the princes sprang to life, and were carried to heaven in chariots of gold.

With a story such as this teaching the benefits the Ganges can confer, it is not to be wondered at that the Hindus wish to die on her banks, and to bathe

BALARĀMA, SUBHADRA, JAGANNĀTHA.

in her stream. To witness the bathing of tens of thousands of pilgrims, and to hear their shout of jubilation as they come up from the water, is an experience never to be forgotten. That a good many of the more intelligent now visit the island as a pleasure trip is true; that the larger number go with the hope of obtaining, by immersion in its waters, the great blessing of pardon from sin, is equally true. And many would willingly die there when the desire of years is gratified, rather than return home and again fall into sin; they could truly say with Simeon, "Lord, now let Thy servant depart in peace."

The next place of pilgrimage is Puri, the scene of Jagannātha's worship; or if the distance is too great, as similar images with their cars are to be seen elsewhere, the people visit one of these minor shrines.

The object of a visit to Puri is to see Jagannātha, as the sight of this deity is said to have the same effect as bathing in the Ganges at Saugar. To see Jagannātha is to cleanse the soul from sin. All other temples are visited with the object of worshipping the idols; but it is to *see* Jagannātha, or rather his image, that is considered the great good.

It is not a difficult thing for the pilgrims to see the image of Jagannātha in the temples where he is worshipped, excepting at Puri, his chief shrine, of which in some respects the other places are but copies, for in the village temples the image is generally visible; but at Puri, it is almost impossible for it to be seen. The explanation is this. The sanctum in which it is kept is quite dark, the image is black, and the pilgrims are not allowed to remain long in front of it, but are hurried along by the temple officials. Before entering the promenade in front of the image, they have to walk round the building two or three times. During this walk, their attention being directed towards the high walls, the glare from the sky on the whitewashed walls is such that when the people enter the temple they can see nothing for a time, and as they pass out have to confess that they could not *see* Jagannātha, and hence their labour in coming has been thrown away. The priests declare that it is because of the enormity of their sins that the vision of the god is withheld. Many of the people having travelled many a weary mile, and spent all their savings for years, have to return without the satisfaction that the sight of this ugly image could give. At certain festivals the people come in tens of thousands to this place, and as the image is then fully exposed to view, they are able to catch sight of it. Many die on the journey to and fro; but there is this consolation for them—the Hindu scriptures distinctly promise that if a pilgrim sets out for Jagannātha's temple and die on the way, he secures all the benefits that would have come to him had he lived until he reached the place.

The image of Jagannātha is anything but attractive. It is an almost shapeless block of wood, with no legs, and stumps only for arms. A legend accounts for this. Centuries ago, as the worship of Vishnu—and Jagannātha is declared to be only another form of Vishnu,—had ceased in the district, a king prayed to the god to appear and re-establish his worship there. The request was acceded to: the god manifested himself to the king, and instructed him to build a temple, and promised to send the architect and builder of the gods to prepare an image, by which he could be always represented upon earth. The king, delighted with this honour, did his part; and when all was ready, Visvakarma, the divine workman, came down and began his work in an enclosure that was protected by high walls from the gaze of the multitude. Not wishing to be seen at his work, the heavenly visitor gave strict orders that he was not to be overlooked as he prepared the idol. For some days his wishes were respected; but at length the curiosity of the king overcame his discretion, and led him to get a ladder that he might have a peep at the great work in progress. But this curiosity was not passed over: the angry deity returned to heaven, leaving the image in its unfinished state. The king was greatly disappointed at first as he saw the shapeless block of wood, but was reassured by Vishnu that, notwithstanding its ugliness, it should still be regarded as his representative. To this day, whenever the idols are renewed at Puri, this ugly model is followed. On the festival days of Jagannātha, gold or silver hands are fixed to the stumps of arms.

Such is the common story. But a more correct view of this worship is that when the Buddhists were driven out of India and their temples destroyed, as their teaching had taken a firm hold of the hearts of many of the people, who were not, however, prepared to give up home and country for its sake, this modified form of Hinduism was adopted in its place; the image of Jagannātha, the lord of the world, being only a modification of certain symbols that were usually found in the Buddhist temples. In the worship of Jagannātha, there are many things very similar indeed to the Buddhistic creed and practice; and it is known that Orissa was for some time the head-quarters of Buddhism.

It is a very noticeable thing that at Puri, Hindus of all castes eat together. In the presence of the god, the caste distinctions that are elsewhere so carefully observed that many would die rather than neglect them, are at the feasts within the temple enclosure quite forgotten; and high and low caste people may be seen partaking together of the rice that has been sanctified by being cooked in this holy place, which to many of the people is the most sacred upon earth.

Ugly, repulsive indeed as the image of Jagannātha is, the deity whom it is supposed to represent was of all the Hindu gods one of the gentlest, and one to whom gods and men are said to have resorted for aid in their times of special need. It is Vishnu the Preserver, not Siva the Destroyer, that is represented; and yet, by some strange error, he is spoken of as the Moloch of India, as one who delights in human blood. Of all the gods in the Hindu Pantheon, Vishnu is *the* one to whom all life is sacred. The followers of Vishnu regard it as sinful to take life even when the victim is sacrificed to Kāli. It may be that the ugly image that is worshipped may have led English people to regard him as cruel; or it may be the accidents that have frequently attended his worship may have given rise to this idea. It is perfectly true that not a year passes by without some people being crushed to death under the wheels of the ponderous cars on which the image is dragged from one temple to another;

but it is equally true that it is not because the Hindu scriptures teach that such sacrifices are pleasing to this deity. It is also true that occasionally men have voluntarily cast themselves under these wheels; but it is because they are weary of life, and imagining that their sins are removed, and fearing lest on their return to ordinary life they should again do evil, they think that it is well to put an end to it at such a holy place. Deaths, mostly accidental, but occasionally voluntary, do occur in connection with the worship of this deity; but the character of the deity represented, and the ordinary worship of his followers, are all opposed to such a course—life in its simplest form being regarded as a most sacred thing by them.

The next great place for pilgrims is Benares. Every Hindu would, if possible, go there once; all would be glad to die there. It is so holy, that whoever dies within the sacred boundaries, whether Hindu, Mahomedan, or Christian, is said to go direct to heaven without waiting for a lengthened stay outside the gates.

Although there are temples sacred to many of the Hindu deities in Benares, it is chiefly Siva, the "Great God" of Hinduism, that is worshipped there; and as he is described as living a life of hardship and suffering, it is thought that physical pain will be pleasing to him. Hence many wishing to obtain his favour are not content to walk many hundreds of miles to visit this place specially dear to him, but for the last few miles they travel in a most painful manner. They throw themselves down at full length on their faces, and having made a mark with their fingers upon the ground, place their toes against this mark and then prostrate themselves again. This process they repeat until they reach the city. I shall never forget the expression of joy that I saw on the faces of many hundreds of people as the city first came within sight. This was the spot towards which their eyes had been turned in anticipation for many years past. Now, at last, their desire was gratified.

As it is accounted a good thing to die in Benares, many of the princes and rich people in distant places have a house within the city, and when growing old, or sickness comes to them, or to any members of their family, if it be possible they are removed, that they may end their days here. On this account, that it is the final resting-place of the religious Hindu, the death-rate is very large. Death in Benares is believed to be a certain entrance to a better and happier life; hence it is not to be wondered at that when men and women feel that the end of their days is at hand, they wish to be taken to this holy city that they may die in the certain hope of heaven, and that their bodies may be burned on the banks of the most purifying stream.

The sacredness of this asylum is not confined to the city proper, but extends to all the land enclosed by a road about fifty miles long, starting from the river bank to another point lower down, though never more than ten miles from the river itself. It is said that any one, whether pure or impure, who dies within this enclosed land is certain to obtain the blessedness of heaven. The inhabitants are supposed to walk along this road once a year to expiate the sins committed; and all the pilgrims must conclude their visit to the city by traversing it. On the journey none excepting the really sick and very young children are allowed to ride. Each must provide his own food and water, and when the journey is over a visit is paid to a a temple, where one of the gods is supposed to act as a recorder to write down the names of the pilgrims who have performed this holy act. Although Benares is accounted a most holy place, and a visit is supposed to effect so great a blessing for its visitors, as a matter of fact few places abound with greater wickedness.

Benares has obtained its pre-eminence as a sin-destroying and peace-giving place from the fact that when Siva cut off the fifth head of Brahmā in a quarrel, it stuck to his hand. Do what he would, he could not get rid of it. Wherever he wandered this head the sign of the evil he had committed against the Brāhmans, of whom Brahmā was the head, was present. But he no sooner entered the precincts of his favourite city, than the head dropped from his hand and he enjoyed peace of mind. As, therefore, Siva got rid of the results of his sin by a visit to this place, it is not surprising that his followers should try to get rid of their sins by similar means.

The other place of pilgrimage I shall notice is Gya. The blessing sought by a visit here is one for the dead, not for the living. Hinduism certainly stands unrivalled in its hold upon the fears of its followers. Each teacher insists on the paramount importance of the duty in which he is personally interested: a man must attend to the lessons of his Guru, or spiritual guide, or he will suffer in hell; he must visit different places of pilgrimage, and there give largely to the temples or he will suffer; he must die on the banks of the Ganges, or his soul cannot be regarded as safe; and he must have descendants to perform his funeral ceremonies for many years after his death, or his salvation is not secured. The system has been elaborated with tremendous skill and cleverness. The chains of superstition are many and strong which bind the Hindu to his gods and compel him to labour for his soul's good.

When a man dies, though the body is burned, the spirit, clothed in a sort of spiritual body, rises into the spirit land; but however good the man may have been, however numerous his religious acts which have earned the blessedness of heaven for perhaps thousands of years, still, unless his funeral rites are properly performed, his soul must wander in misery, unable to enter heaven. Certain offerings of cakes, &c., must be made by his son, in order that the deceased may join the company of the blessed. From ten to thirty days these gifts are presented daily; then monthly for a year; and then yearly for two or three generations. It is promised that if the cakes are offered at Gya, not only the deceased himself, but his ancestors for many generations, and also the offerer himself, will assuredly enter into the enjoyment of the blessedness of heaven immediately after death. Offerings to ancestors are made at all the great festivals, but one visit to Gya on behalf of a dead person is supposed to be sufficient. With such promises it is only natural that a loving son should willingly undertake this journey, and do his best to secure his father's happiness; and that a Hindu should be anxious to have a son who would be willing to incur the expense of these services. Long before the doctrine of Purgatory had been taught in

Catholic countries, the Hindus had elaborated the system which makes the salvation of the dead largely depend upon the gifts and acts of the living.

As the sacred water from the Ganges is considered

HINDU CARRYING HOLY WATER FROM THE GANGES.

an acceptable offering to the gods, men earn their living by carrying it, sometimes from immense distances, and selling it to the devout Hindus for this purpose.

CHAPTER IX.

RELIGIOUS FESTIVALS.

The life of the ordinary Hindus is very monotonous. They have no Sunday with its rest from work, its church services, its happy and pleasant associations. For weeks, and sometimes months, together, excepting on the market days when it is necessary for them to go to a neighbouring village, there is the same round of commonplace routine duties. There are no lectures, no concerts, and no amusements, excepting those connected with religion, of which I am now about to speak. Certainly it is true in India that "all work and no play *has* made Jack a dull boy." For, as compared with ourselves, the Hindu is a calm and stolid being, with very little fun in him. These festivals take the place of church services, concerts, theatres, and are a combination of the three.

Just as in England we have Christmas Day and Good Friday to bring to mind the birth and death of our Lord, the Hindu has a special day to commemorate the birth of Krishna and other important events of his life, and other days on which Siva's life on earth is especially remembered. And just as we have our saints' days, *e.g.*, St. John, St. Matthew,

THE CAR OF JAGANNĀTHA.

&c., the Hindu has days specially sacred to some of the other gods, such as Durgā, Sarasvati, Lakshmi, &c. And it is largely by this means that the people are taught the stories about the many gods and goddesses they worship. It is a noticeable fact that, although most of the people cannot read, taken as a whole they know far more about Hinduism than the masses in England know about Jesus Christ and the Old and New Testament saints.

These festivals are commonly held in the courtyard of a Hindu house; or, in the villages where there is no yard large enough for the purpose, a temporary building of matting is erected, which is removed when the festival is over. Some of these festivals are held in the neighbourhood of a temple; but these are not very common.

In the courtyard of every large Hindu mansion, immediately opposite to the entrance gate is a platform which is called the "god's room," and on this the image is placed for worship on festival days—the family idol being kept in a less public room. It is taught that whoever incurs the expense of having a religious festival in his house, by that act purchases the forgiveness of a certain number of sins. In principle, this does not largely differ from the indulgences granted by the Pope, against which Martin Luther thundered so powerfully. When, therefore, a gentleman determines to have one of these services, his first duty is to order the image. These are made of various sizes, according to the price agreed upon; some of them being only about two feet high, others being almost as big as Goliath. The workman first makes a framework of bamboo, on which he ties some sacred grass. Upon this he lays mud from the Ganges, which he moulds into the desired figure. This is dried in the sun, painted and robed; so then, when it is brought home, it looks like a very pretty or a very ugly doll, according as it is the representation of Durgā or of Kāli.

When the image is fixed, a priest is appointed to perform the worship—for the language always used in worship is the Sanskrit, which few even of the priests now understand. They can read or repeat the words, though many of them are too ignorant to know their meaning. No one but a priest is allowed to make an offering to the gods; before the family idol, a priest must perform all the ceremonies. In the morning the religious ceremonies occupy about a couple of hours, and about the same time in the evening; but though a few curious people may stand for a minute or two to watch the priest perform his part, as a rule neither the gentleman on whose behalf the service is held, nor any of the people of the house or neighbourhood, remain long. This is the priest's work—they have no share in it.

One of the most interesting parts of this ceremonial is what is called "the giving of life" to the image. Until this is done the idol is regarded as simply mud, &c.; but when it is finished it is believed to be divine, and none but Hindus would be allowed to go within a few yards of it. The festival may continue for one, two, or three days, at the end of which "farewell" is taken of the god, and the image is again treated as mud, and is carried to the river side, where it is placed on a couple of boats lashed together. The boats are rowed out into the stream, accompanied with bands of music and torches, the lashing is cut, the boats separate, the image falls into the stream, and the worship of this particular deity is over for a year.

But though the people take no part in the worship proper, they come in crowds to the amusements that are provided during the night. The gentleman of the house generally gives a feast to his friends after the evening worship is concluded, and then the amusements begin. These take place in the middle of the courtyard, immediately in front of the image, and are supposed to be provided for the god's amusement as much as for that of the people. A small space is marked off with poles, in which the performance takes place, the crowds accommodating themselves in the space outside this enclosure, packed like herrings in a barrel.

These amusements are of the most varied kind. Frequently there are bands of musicians, with men and women singers, when the performance takes more the character of a concert. But any one expecting to hear anything approaching English music would be terribly disappointed. Almost every Bengali singer —and I have heard some of the best—sings through his nose, and a disagreeable nasal sound is most conspicuous in the performance. As a rule the songs are of a very objectionable character, descriptive of the sayings and doings of deities who were as bad as, and often far worse than, any of the people who worship them. The shouting—shrieking is perhaps the better word—which goes on all the night, from about 11 p.m. to 7 or 8 a.m., lives in the memory for many years after.

But *the* attraction to most people is the Jātra, *i.e.* a sort of religious drama. Companies of actors (no actresses), dressed to represent the gods and goddesses and their attendants, perform plays illustrating the lives of the deities, according to the teaching of the scriptures. The words and gestures are often of a very immoral kind. Between the acts there is dancing and singing by professional performers. It is wonderful to see the interest the people manifest in the stories of the lives of their gods. They remain spell-bound the whole night, as the actors—sometimes fairly good, generally very poor indeed—try to represent the heavenly rulers. Generally there is a great deal of fun caused by an actor who takes the part of Nārada, a sort of demi-god who was a general tale-bearer and mar-plot. These plays do not need a stage, but are performed on the ground; there is no scenery—the actors when not engaged keep their seats, and rise when their turn comes to speak.

In some places, instead of a Jātra, dancing girls perform; and in the cities it has become common to engage a European company from the theatre to play a farce, or a circus company to ride! This is all in the immediate presence of the idol.

As there are two or three festivals a month, excepting during the rainy season, it will be impossible to attempt a description of all. I can give a brief account of a few only of the more important.

The Jagannātha festivals are three in number, there being an interval of about a fortnight between the first and second, and between the second and third.

1. *The Snān Jātra, or Bathing Festival.*

Puri, a town on the sea-coast of Orissa, is the head-quarters of this worship. Year by year over a hundred thousand pilgrims set out from their homes to be present at this festival; but, owing to the exposure and privations of the journey, hundreds perish by the way in going or returning. The expenses of travelling to and living at Puri are so great, that some die of starvation on the return journey, whilst many beg their food as they travel. As, however, there are images of the deity in many places, and the ritual at Puri is carefully followed, those who cannot undertake the long journey to Orissa content themselves with a visit to a village nearer home where the festivals are observed.

The Snān Jatra is a festival in which the idol is bathed in public. On a high platform, around which from eighty to a hundred thousand people are assembled, the priests go through the ceremony of bathing the image of the Lord of the world. As the ceremony proceeds there is the greatest solemnity amongst the crowd of spectators; but when the signal is given that it is completed, the cry of "Jai, jai, Jagannātha!" ("Victory, victory to Jagannātha!"), bursts forth with such fulness of sound that it can never be forgotten. Of all the ceremonies of Hinduism that I have seen, this is by far the most impressive. As soon as the bathing of the image is over, the people wander about amongst the stalls, and business and pleasure rule the day.

The exposure during the bath is supposed to give fever to the god, so for a fortnight the temple doors are closed. During this time, as the image has become discoloured owing to the flowers, water, &c., that have been thrown upon it in the course of the year, it receives a fresh coat of paint; so that, when it is brought to view at the Car Festival, it is resplendent in its new colours.

2. *The Rath Jātra, or Car Festival.*

As it is supposed that the fever has weakened the deity, fourteen days after his bath the image is taken from the temple, hauled upon a ponderous car and dragged to the temple of some other god, with whom it remains for a fortnight for change of air. I should mention that Jagannātha is generally attended by images of his brother, Balarāma, and his sister, Subhadra. These cars are made after one model, though varying in size according to the wealth and taste of their owners. They have sixteen wheels of solid wood, and some of the cars are as high as two or three-storeyed houses. To these cars thick cables are attached, and thousands of the people gladly assist in hauling, as it is said that heavenly rewards await those who lay hold of the rope. At Puri a number of villagers receive their lands rent free on condition that they help in dragging the car; whilst the prince of the district rejoices in the title of "Sweeper of the temple of Jagannātha."

The cars having remained in one place for a year, and there being no means of guiding them, when they begin to move they go with a rush: it is in this manner that accidents occur, although there are large numbers of police in attendance to keep the road clear. Any one seeing the ceremony, and witnessing the excitement of the crowd, would not wonder that occasionally some of the people should be crushed to death. But as was said before, the crushing of people is not a recognized part of the ceremony, nor is there anything in the character of the god to lead the people to imagine that the sacrifice of a human life would be acceptable to him; his worship tends rather to its preservation than to its destruction.

3. *The Ulta Rath, or Return of the Car.*

This festival is not by any means so popular as the others and attracts far fewer people. After a visit of a fortnight, the image is again placed upon the car and taken back to its own temple; but it often happens that men have to be paid before they assist in pulling the car on its homeward journey.

The Durgā Puja.

In Bengal the Durgā festival is perhaps the most popular of all, as there the female deities are more generally worshipped than in other parts of India. It is a singular fact that where woman is the least trusted, the worship of the goddesses should be so common. Durgā, the wife of Siva, the great god, is worshipped under many forms, as it is taught that although her husband continued to live on earth without forsaking his body by death, she died and returned to earth several times; but somehow or other she always managed to win back the affections of her husband. First she came as Úmā, then as Parvati, which life she destroyed because angry with her father for slighting her husband; and then as Kāli, Durgā, and a host of other names, for the destruction of demons, the hereditary enemies of the gods. The name Durgā was assumed by her because she slew a demon named Durga. How it is that during this great conflict she was at one time the fearful Kāli with her ugly black face, and also the golden Durgā with her ten arms, I cannot say. But such is the teaching of the books.

This festival is called the Christmas of Bengal, because of the great family gatherings that are connected with it. Government offices, banks, and the houses of business generally, are wholly or partially closed for twelve days. This long holiday enables the working members of a family who have been living at a distance to visit their homes, and see again the faces of wife and children. When it is remembered that many of the educated men do not take their wives to live with them if their employment is at a distance from home, but leave them in the care of father or brother, it will be understood what an immense boon this prolonged holiday proves. At the Durgā Puja, all who can possibly manage it are present at the old home.

The worship of Durgā is similar to that of other deities already described. Images are made for the occasion and placed in the courtyards of the houses; amusements are provided for all who come, and goats are sacrificed to her. At no festival connected with Vishṇu in any of his forms is life taken; but goats and buffaloes are supposed to be an acceptable gift to Durgā. When this happy-looking image is put into its place, and the lamps of the courtyard lighted, it certainly presents a most attractive appearance. As the many hands of the goddess are filled with warlike weapons, and she is standing on a lion with a demon dying at her feet, there certainly seems some incongruity between her face and her surroundings. As the feast is made in nearly every large house in Calcutta, and the Hindus pace the streets in crowds, going from house to house to see the amusements, it is a noticeable fact that the police have scarcely anything to do except to prevent the blocking of the streets by keeping the carriages and crowds moving. The noise of the music in the native part of the town is so great that sleep is almost impossible.

The Dōl Jātra is a festival connected with Krishna, that is an occasion for a great deal of amusement. On this occasion the images of the deity are placed in swings, to commemorate the pleasure Krishna enjoyed in the swing during his residence on earth. Jātras, dancing, and amusements of all kinds are provided, the image of the god being placed in the midst that he may enjoy it all.

It will be noticed that although these are religious feasts, the people generally have no part whatever in the religious ceremonies. They see the image and prostrate themselves before it; but even the gentlemen who arrange for them have no share in the worship. The Hindu system provides for a division of labour: it is the duty of the priests to perform the religious ceremonies; it is the duty of the people to pay them for doing it.

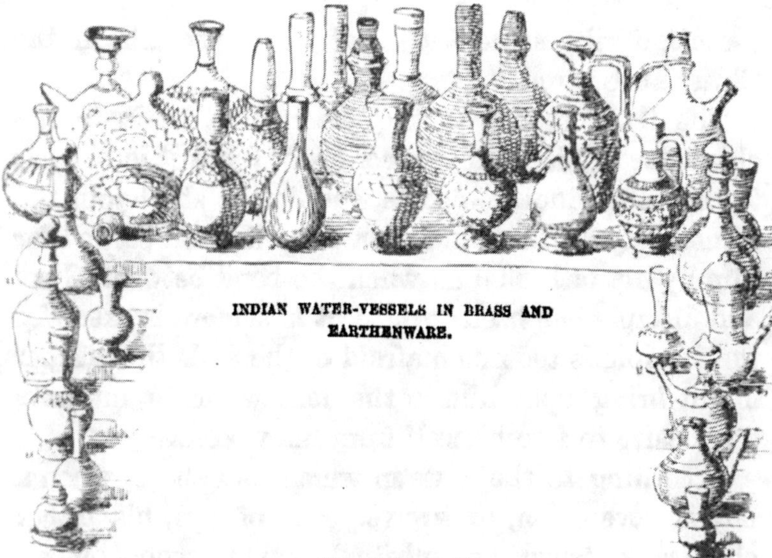

INDIAN WATER-VESSELS IN BRASS AND EARTHENWARE.

CHAPTER X.

GURUS, OR RELIGIOUS TEACHERS, AND THEIR DISCIPLES.

It is very interesting as we become acquainted with the different forms of religion that have been embraced by men, to see the same fundamental ideas though expressed in a somewhat different manner. Man is everywhere the same, and as the object of his religion is to unite him to his deities, and to lead him to do what will please them, the means employed are very similar. Hence we find in Hinduism a form of initiation almost identical in object with confirmation in the Churches of Rome and of England, and joining the church amongst the Non-conformists. Up to a certain time the individual is outside the pale of the church; but after his formal reception he is regarded as an integral part of it. Although the form of reception is somewhat peculiar in Hinduism, in spirit it is essentially the same with that which prevails in the Christian Church.

The Guru stands to the disciple in India in the character of his pastor or confessor; but it is not left to the individual to decide whether he shall join the community of the Hindus or not—it is all settled for him by his father: and when the bond between Guru and disciple has been formed, it is seldom broken, for the disciple is too much afraid of the evils the teacher might bring upon him in the next world to intimate any desire to free himself from his yoke.

According to the caste in which he is born, when a boy is seven, ten, or twelve years of age, his father chooses a Guru or spiritual guide, who, on an auspicious day, comes to initiate the young disciple—to admit him into the fellowship of the Hindu system. When the boy has been duly bathed and clothed in spotlessly clean clothes, the teacher takes him aside and teaches him a mantra or text in which the name of one of the gods occurs. As a rule these texts are destitute of meaning, and are simply a string of words that the boy can easily remember. This text must be kept secret, fearful penalties being threatened if they repeat the words in the hearing of any one. I have known Christians hesitate to repeat the text they had been taught at this time, even when they have separated themselves from the Hindu community.

In many of the sects it is the duty of the members to repeat this text a hundred and eight times every day; and as a help in counting, they carry rosaries or strings of seeds, similar to those used by Roman Catholics as they repeat their Ave Marias and Paternosters. Some of the people possessed by a Pharisaic spirit place their beads in a bag, but this bag they do not hesitate to hold conspicuously in front of them; and as they repeat their text and move their fingers along the beads, they seem to say to the bystanders, "See how regular I am in my devotions, and also how humble and unostentatious." The spirit of the Pharisees is not at all confined to the Jews and Christians; it is to be found in some form or other all the world over.

To the sons of the Hindus belonging to the highest castes, but especially to the Brāhmans, this initiation is a most important ceremony, as they then put on the poitra, or sacred thread, for the first time. This poitra is simply a few strains of thread worn round the neck, or rather hanging from the left shoulder; but it is the mark of spiritual aristocracy. No peer of the realm of Britain is prouder of his birth than is the poorest Brāhman in Bengal; and no sovereign values his crown more highly than does the high-caste man, however humble his position, esteem the privilege of wearing this thread. It commands the respect, almost the worship, of the millions of the lower castes; and it gives him the right to know the Vedas, the most sacred book of the Hindus, the knowledge of which forms the passport to the highest bliss of heaven. The high-caste people in India enjoy the profoundest respect of men, and they only in the present life have any hope of gaining the greatest good to which man can aspire. The low-caste people hope in due course to attain to a similar position, it is true, but hundreds of thousands of years may pass before this position can be secured. The thread once put on is never taken off. In the case of Brāhman converts, the taking off of the poitra is considered as the final abandoning of Hinduism.

It is a noticeable fact, that after the thread is worn its possessors are spoken of as *twice born*—a term almost identical with that used by Jesus as given in John iii. 7, "Ye must be born again," the investiture with the poitra being commonly spoken of as a second "*birth*." I remember once when I had been preaching to a crowd of Hindus on the text just mentioned, that a Brāhman came up to me smiling as he said, "I agree, sir, with all that you have been saying; I find that Hinduism and Christianity after all are the same." He had heard me insist upon the necessity of the new birth, but this one idea had so astonished and delighted him that he had not listened to my explanation of the term. He said, "Yes, yes, you are right; all men must be born again, *i.e.* become Brāhmans before they can enter into the kingdom of heaven."

When a Guru by the teaching of the mantra, and in the case of the higher castes by putting on the poitra, has initiated a disciple into Hinduism, it is his duty to visit him from time to time to give him his blessing and to impart religious knowledge. In some cases there can be no doubt that a real attempt is made to improve these occasions by teaching passages from some of the scriptures. I have often seen and heard them at their work. But generally their visit is simply for the purpose of extorting a good gift. Some of these men have no home, but spend their time in the houses of their disciples, going from one to another, and staying with them for weeks at a time. In books written by Hindus there are strange scenes described, in which these visits are highly ridiculed. The man comes in state, but his advent is regarded with anything but joy. The best room in the house is given up to him, the best food that can be purchased is freely prepared for him, and then comes the talk about his present. He ridicules the offer first made, which, like that of a would-be purchaser, is very low, but which is gradually raised, whilst his demands are lessened; until at last a bargain is struck, and having obtained as much as he can get, he condescends to bless his trembling disciple, and passes on to fleece some one else. When it is remembered that the Hindu books teach that the blessing of the Guru secures the salvation of his disciples, whilst his curse effects their damnation, it is not to be wondered at that they freely give whatever he demands, in order that they may keep on good terms with him. Some of their books distinctly teach that it is better to offend the gods than the Gurus; for if a man offend a god, his Guru can intercede for him; but if he offend his Guru, no one can help him.

When we bear in mind the fact that most of the people are unable to read, and, further, that many of the sacred books are in Sanskrit, an unknown tongue even to those who have received an ordinary education, it is easy to see how dependent the people are upon these teachers. They have no Sunday-school teachers, no town missionaries, no district visitors, no churches wherein religious instruction can be obtained. Hinduism does not lead men to care at all for the spiritual welfare of their neighbours; in men of their own caste a little interest may be felt, but certainly not for those outside of it. It is to these spiritual guides they look for instruction.

Perhaps once a year, occasionally oftener, they receive a visit, hear a few words read from one of the books, and its teaching explained. I have often, in preaching, astonished the people by calling attention to passages in their own scriptures of which they were perfectly ignorant. Some years ago, tracts were written giving an account of several of the Hindu deities, with quotations from the sacred writings; whilst, at the same time, the evil of worshipping these beings was pointed out. The people most eagerly took these books, crowding upon the missionaries to obtain them, because they gave far clearer teaching respecting the idols than the people could obtain elsewhere. It was felt at last by some that these tracts rather hindered than helped Christian work, although they were written with the main object of leading the people to Christ.

As a specimen of what these Gurus teach, I will mention what I heard one of them read to his disciples. He had about half a dozen men sitting round eagerly listening to every word that fell from his lips. He began by telling the people that the name of Krishna should often be upon their lips, because the mere repetition of that name was pleasing to him, and would ensure their entrance into heaven however evil their life might have been, even the messengers of Yama, the Judge, being obliged to do his bidding. There was once living on earth a very wicked woman who had daily amused herself by teaching her parrot to repeat the name of Krishna. At length the time came for her to die. As she had lived, so she died, a wicked woman, feeling no sorrow for her sin, no repentance, no change of life. When her spirit left her body, it was seized by Yama's officers; and as it was being dragged before him for punishment, Krishna's messengers snatched the woman away and carried her to Krishna's heaven, where she was at once received, and entered upon the enjoyment of its pleasures.

He read a similar story of a man who had a son named Nārāyana, one of the many names of Vishnu. When this man was dying, as he wanted a little water to drink, he called his son, "Nārāyana, Nārāyana;" and as the name crossed his lips, he fell back dead. There was no thought of the god in his heart, the name only being on his lips; but this fact was so pleasing to the deity, that in like manner he rescued him from judgment and gave him a place in heaven.

It is by stories such as these that the people are led to believe that the doing of certain acts will ensure their happiness after death. The continued repetition of the names of the gods is a most common practice. They think they shall be heard for their much speaking, but have yet to learn that God, as a loving Father, waits to hear His children's prayer. Surely people in this condition are as "sheep without a shepherd," and should move our hearts to compassion as the heart of the Saviour was moved as He saw the condition of the people of Palestine.

CHAPTER XI.

HINDU SAINTS.

Hinduism is a most elastic and comprehensive system of religion. It provides a small round of simple duties for those who do not care to give much time to religion, and it also regards with favour those who wish to devote all their days to it.

In the olden time, when the founders of Hinduism came into India, they taught that as it was the duty of the warrior-caste to rule and protect the nation, of the merchants to buy and sell, and of the servants to minister to the wants of all the rest, it was the duty of the Brāhmans to attend to religion and to perform religious ceremonies for all the rest. Concerning this priestly caste, it ordered that their lives should be divided into four parts; they were first to be students, learning from the older men the sacred compositions that had not at that time been written; they were then to marry and take care of their home and perform religious ceremonies: then they were to be teachers, handing down to others the words of wisdom they had learned; and then they were to retire from their families and, by quiet meditation and thought, prepare for death and entrance into heaven.

Most marvellous stories are written of the immense

power these men gained over their fellow-mortals, and even over the gods, by their religious merit and the sacred texts they had learned. At length their position was declared to be such that the gods even were bound to obey their commands.

This belief in the immense power to be obtained by a religious life has led many Brāhmans and, as changes

A HINDU SAINT.

in Hinduism crept in, many who were not Brāhmans, to assume the garb and profession of ascetics or saints. Almost all the many sects has its order of sainthood; and many men, young and old, partly from the honour in which they are held, and partly with a desire to obtain greater bliss in heaven, have forsaken home and family to live a life of religion, to become Sādhus, or saints, as they are called.

From what I have seen of these men, I confess I have not very great respect for them; for certainly they differ as widely as possible from the Christian idea of sainthood. Still it cannot be denied that amongst the Hindus they are generally held in the highest esteem. Gautama Buddha, the founder of Buddhism, and Chaitanya, the great reformer in Bengal, were Sādhus; and certainly the self-sacrifice that is apparent in their lives added great weight to the lessons they taught. In fact, most of the great religious changes that have occurred in India have been largely effected by men who were professed saints. But it is not of the few who were eminently pure in their lives and sincere in their efforts to benefit men that I am now writing, but of the many who, as far as one can judge, are living useless, or even injurious, lives.

The saints of to-day—and they are counted by millions—do no work, they do not teach, they do good to no one. Their lives are spent in wandering from temple to temple, from shrine to shrine, to receive the gifts of the pious. They are religious beggars, and nothing more. In appearance, as a rule, they are most repulsive. They go about the country almost if not entirely naked, their bodies being smeared over with ashes. They never sleep in a house, but under trees or in the verandahs of temples. Many of them never bathe, nor do they comb out their long hair, which lies matted upon their heads. Once I had my tent in the midst of five hundred of them for about three days, and was heartily glad for some reasons when we parted company. As they sit huddled over a small fire in the cold air, they look the picture of misery; and as many of them smoke opium and eat hemp, they have a most idiotic stare. A more aimless life than that which these "holy" men live, it would be impossible to conceive.

Some of these are the worshippers of Vishnu, and as that deity is said to have been fond of amusement, his saints have a fairly comfortable life compared with that which is endured by the worshippers of Siva. This deity is described as living a life of penance or suffering; hence those who profess to be his followers make their lives as miserable as they can. Physical pain is supposed to be an acceptable offering to him; and many of the "saints" of Siva live a life of pain. I have seen men who have held up one arm, and others both arms, until the muscles have shrunk so that they cannot move them; others who have stood on one leg for years; others who have gazed into the burning sun until they have become blind; others who have sworn to be silent, and who appear to have lost the power of speech. There are some who sit helpless as children, and will not eat unless they are fed. More miserable specimens of humanity it would be hard to meet with in the most wretched slums of Europe. Yet these are considered by the Hindus as ideal men; those who are by this means pleasing God, and becoming fit for the enjoyment of His pure presence.

Often I have tried to converse with them, but generally found it a hopeless task. Many of them, either through real mental weakness, or as a result of the opium they had taken, seemed to have lost the power of thinking; an idiotic stare, or an unintelligible grunt, was about all I could get from them in reply. These are the modern examples of the thousands of monks who in the early ages of Christianity withdrew from the world that, as they thought, they could serve God the better: a conception as opposed to the example and teaching of Jesus as one could possibly imagine.

Of course it must not be supposed that the great majority of these men are all that they appear: that many are there is no doubt. But if all one hears of them is true, a large number of them are amongst the worst of men. On certain days when festivals in honour of Siva are held, many of the working classes assume the dress and profession of saints for a time. Daubed with ashes, almost naked, and in a state of intoxication, they beg from house to house. Some of them throw themselves down from platforms eight feet high upon knives; others used to swing from high bamboo poles with hooks fixed in their bodies. But this practice has now been stopped by the Government. This was all done in the belief that it was pleasing to the god Siva.

CHAPTER XII.

BURNING GHĀTS AND TREATMENT OF THE DYING.

In few respects does Hinduism present a greater contrast to Christianity than in the treatment of the sick and dying. When in England a person is ill, and it is feared that death is near, words of hope are spoken to cheer, all noise is prevented lest they should be disturbed, and every attention is paid so that, if possible, their life may be prolonged; or if that cannot be, that their departure may be as free from pain and anxiety as possible. But in India the very opposite to this is the rule.

Now it would be very wrong to imagine that the Hindus are cruel, or that they love their friends less than we love ours. It is because they love them, and hope by this means to secure their highest good, that, taught by their religion, they act in a cruel manner. No English son is more tender in his love to his mother, or more dutiful and respectful to his father, than are most Hindus to their parents. I have heard sons speak to their parents in England as I have never heard Hindus speak to theirs. I mention this because the treatment of the dying seems to be most unnatural. The fault lies, not in the absence of kindly

BURNING GHÂT.

feeling on the part of the people, but in the system of religion which teaches and enforces these practices.

When a man is sick, and the medical attendant is of opinion that the case is hopeless, he intimates this to the son or some member of the family, who immediately makes arrangements for his speedy removal from the house. It is regarded ceremonially defiling for a dead body to remain in a house, and it is believed that if a man die on the banks of the Ganges or some other sacred stream, he will be certain to obtain a speedy entrance into heaven. In order, then, to save the living from defilement and to secure the greatest good of the dying, the Hindus are impelled to act in a manner very different from that to which their kindly feelings would prompt.

When the arrangements are made for carrying the sick man away, the fact is intimated to him that he should "go and see Ganga" (the Ganges). It may be that up to this time he had no idea that death was near; but this hint tells him that his friends have now no hope of his recovery. Often this fact in itself is sufficient to lead a man whose mind and body are weakened by disease to despair, and this despair certainly renders him all the more likely to die. The bright and cheerful faces of the attendants of the sick, and the kind and cheery words of the medical attendants, have often done as much for the recovery of the patients as the medicines they have taken. This treatment has enabled many who otherwise would have succumbed to arise strong and well from what might otherwise have been their death-bed. But in India words of despair rather than of hope are spoken whenever the doctor may consider the patient will die. In cases where European physicians are called in to see a patient, I need hardly say that such advice would not be given.

Before its removal from the house, the wife and other female members of the household crowd round the cot on which the invalid is lying, and as they have no hope of again seeing their loved one, the parting is a most heartrending scene. The tears and shrieks of the women in their supreme moment of sorrow must necessarily add to the sorrow and distress of the sick man. Of course, where the female members of a family are kept in seclusion, none of the ladies go down to the riverside with the dying man; their last sight of him is as he is being carried away from the comforts of home to die on the banks of the river.

When the last farewell is spoken, the bed is quickly carried to the river. In some places an open shed is there to receive the sick in their dying moments; but generally there is no such place: the cot is placed on the ground underneath a tree, and there the dying pass their last moments, or, as it sometimes happens, their last weeks. I have seen some who for twenty-one days have been awaiting death, left sometimes for hours together without any one near to speak to them or to give them a drop of water to moisten their parched tongue. Exposed to the heat by day and the cold and damp at night, those who with proper care at home might probably have recovered pass away. Added to all this exposure, instead of the quiet and comfort of home and the presence of those they have loved best, they see other poor creatures like themselves awaiting the advent of death, the great ender ot their woes. In years gone by, if a man recovered when he had been carried to the holy stream he was not allowed to return to his home, but, like the lepers of Israel, had to live with others in a separate village, who, because death did not take them when it was expected, were declared to be "rejected of the goddess." But at the present time, if the end is not quick enough the dying are often carried into the river and placed up to their waist in the water, and mud thrust into their mouths to hasten their death. All this is done because the Hindu scriptures promise great good in the next world to those who die in or near the sacred streams.

If you were to question some of these people about to die, as to their state of mind in reference to the future, it would be found to be quite as pitiable as their bodily surroundings. Ask them where they are going, and what their condition after death will be, and any Christian heart would be saddened by the answer of despair that would come. Most of them, at any rate, would answer, "We are leaving this life, but where we are going we cannot tell, nor whether our condition will be one of happiness or misery. If in this life we have done well, we shall go to heaven, to receive the reward of our good deeds; and when that is over, we must return again to the world in a higher caste than our present one, and then have another life here. If in this life our evil deeds outnumber our good ones, we shall sink into hell, there receive the appointed punishment, and then come again into the world in a lower caste than our present one. But God only knows which of these two courses is before us!" Comfort, peace, there cannot be with such a belief. Indeed, the Hindu scriptures distinctly say that the blessed in heaven often suffer sorrow, as they remember that their bliss there must come to an end, and they be born on earth again to toil and suffer, and, it may be, through sin, sink back to the bottom of the ladder, a whole life being spent in rising a single step. They believe that in the end they will reach the top, and return to God, the great ocean of which their spirit is as a single drop; but it may take millions of years before this can be attained. My heart has bled often as I have seen these people crossing the valley of the shadow of death in such gross darkness, without a single ray to illuminate its darkness; feeling no friendly hand to support them in the hour of human helplessness.

Immediately the breath has left the body, preparations are made for burning it. Cremation in England in a properly constructed furnace is one thing, but cremation as it is carried on in India is quite another. I have no objection to the plan as it is carried out here, and for many reasons think it desirable that it should become common; but a Burning Ghāt in India certainly has not much to recommend it. To the Hindu, however, with his present views, it seems all that can be desired; for when the Calcutta Municipality erected a furnace something like the one at Woking, the people refused to use it, and so the good intentions of the ruling powers of the city were fruitless.

In Calcutta and the suburbs there are several Burning Ghāts, *i.e.* simple enclosures with four walls by the river-side. Sailing up the river many fires are visible, as bodies may be burned anywhere the friends choose; it is only in and near the cities that any restrictions are made. The people who die near the Ganges are burned on its banks; or if they die at a distance, all who can afford it carry the dead bodies of their friends to the nearest part of that river. But as many are too poor for this, they burn them on the banks of the nearest stream, and are content with taking a small part of the body to throw into the more holy water of the Ganges.

The process of burning is a very simple one. A heap of wood is first prepared, on which the body, covered with a clean sheet, is laid. Over the body a little more wood is placed, and upon this a little ghī, or clarified butter, is poured to make it burn briskly. The son or nearest relation, after walking round the pile seven times, sets fire to it; the priest at the ghāt having first repeated certain texts, without which the burning would not be considered as satisfactorily accomplished. The Hindus worship Fire under the name of Agni, and the burden of the priest's text is a prayer to Agni that as the fire consumes the earthly body of the deceased person, he will convey the spiritual part to the heavenly mansions.

As, however, many of the people are too poor to obtain a sufficient quantity of wood entirely to consume the body, very frequently portions are left. These are eagerly devoured by the jackals, kites, vultures, wild dogs, and crows. An ordinary Burning Ghāt in India is a sight that remains indelibly impressed upon the memory. If boys in England fear to cross a churchyard at night lest ghosts should appear, it certainly is not to be wondered at that

Hindu boys and grown-up people too should prefer to go a mile or two out of their way rather than pass some of these places at night. I confess that at times I have felt a little "creepy" as I heard the four-footed carrion animals gnawing at the body of some human being, who but a few hours before had been living amongst his fellows. And I can now see with the mind's eye some sad, sad sights at the river-side. I have seen a father carry the dead body of his only son, who was dear to him as mine to me, and there with his own hands prepare the wood, set fire to the pile, and stand by until that lovely form was reduced to ashes. I have seen the son perform this sad office for mother and father, who were loved as warmly as mother and father are loved in England. And there was this sorrow added to any that we may suffer: they have no hope of meeting again those whom they have loved and lost. To the Hindu the separation caused by death is an eternal separation; there is no hope of a united family group in heaven. In their next appearances on earth, father and son, mother and daughter, may be entirely unknown to each other. Some members of the same family may rise in the ladder to the supreme bliss; others may sink. Stories are to be found of men who have accidentally found a father in some animal form. Here is one. A great and good king, tired of life, presented himself at the gate of heaven with a dog, who had been his companion and friend for many years. On being told that though his good deeds entitled him to enter heaven, his dog could not be permitted to accompany him, "Then," said the king, "I will go to hell." To hell he went, and when taken before Yama, the judge, the king told the story of his not being admitted to heaven. "Oh," said Yama, "this was simply to try your constancy; that dog is your father, and, as you have proved yourself worthy, you and he can now enter upon the enjoyment of heavenly bliss." Upon this the dog resumed its human form, and father and son were welcomed into heaven. The blessed truths that Jesus has taught of life and immortality, the Hindu has yet to learn.

In the following account of the death and cremation of Sir Jung Bahadur, which took place outside of British India, we have the last instance that I have known of what at one time was common in Bengal, viz., the burning of the living wives with the corpse of their husband. This happened only about ten years ago. The account is taken from a correspondent to a Calcutta newspaper:—

"The 25th of February last was a holy day, and His Excellency, Sir Jung Bahadur, wanted to bathe in the Bagmittee. He reached Pathuriaghat for that purpose, and, before sunrise, entered the river for the purpose of bathing. He was in the highest spirits all along, and there was no symptom whatever of approaching death. After performing his ablutions, he sat on the bank to perform the usual *pooja* (worship). He was soon after seen to be motionless, and his followers found that his life was extinct. There was bitter wailing amongst his followers, and his private secretary at once sent an express to the capital. From the capital a strict order reached the camp at Pathuriaghat to postpone his funeral rites, and soon after his three principal Ranees (queens), brother, and son reached the spot.

The three Ranees expressed a desire of sacrificing themselves in the funeral pile of their husband. The son said nothing; the brother of the deceased, however, tried to dissuade them, but they were not to be dissuaded. So heaps of sandal wood, resin, and a large quantity of *ghi*, and other materials were procured. When all these arrangements were made, the ladies bathed in the river, performed their *pooja*, and made presents of cows, elephants, horses, and gold to Brāhmans and holy men. Their next step was to take proper measures for the government of the country and the maintenance of peace. Some officers were promoted, others confirmed in their posts, and some general directions given to their brother-in-law. Their last act was to release some prisoners. The funeral pile was then ready, and they entered it unconcernedly, all the while muttering prayers. The corpse was then laid upon his back, and the ladies disposed of themselves in this way. The eldest placed the head upon her lap, and the two others took charge of the feet. They were then surrounded by fuel and odorous combustibles. While the Ranees gazed upon the features of their husband, as if utterly forgetful of every other consideration, fire was applied by the son of the deceased, and the crowd burst into tears. All was over in the course of a few minutes."

As an illustration of the common belief in the transmigration of souls, *i.e.* of the spirit of a man reappearing on earth in the form of an animal, the following account of the ruler of Cashmere may be given. This describes the belief prevailing at this very time in India :—

"The telegraph has announced the death of H. H.

Runbeer Singh, G.C.S.I., Maharajah of Jummoo and Cashmere. He was the ruler of Jummoo as well as of Cashmere; and the town of Jummoo on the Tavee might be called his capital, for he lived at that place a great deal more than in Srinuggur. Runbeer Singh was a Hindu, and having none of our troops or officials, except a Resident, in his country, he has been able to enforce the rule against killing the sacred cow; owing to this law, all visitors to Cashmere soon discover that roast beef does not belong to the delights of the Happy Valley. It is said that the Maharajah had a strong desire to visit England, but his Hindu education and feelings prevented him. His reason was that he had heard that the flesh of the cow was exposed in shops for sale in London, and with the chances of having to see such sights, which to his mind were so horrible and repulsive, he would not risk coming to this country. This is a very curious illustration of the power of training and habit. When Gulab Singh, the father of the late Maharajah, died, the Brāhmans and Pundits declared that he had passed by the process of the Metempsychosis into the body of a fish. Now the lakes of Cashmere, as well as the rivers and the canals, are full of fish, and owing to this belief no one was allowed to catch them, lest the Maharajah might be taken and eaten. Europeans were exempt from this command, and to Hindus, who as a rule do not eat fish, it was no privation; but to the Mohamedan part of the population it was a great hardship, particularly as fish are so plentiful. At a place called Mutton, where there is one of the sources of the Jhelum, the water comes into a tank, which is full of sacred fish, one of which is supposed to be the representative of Gulab Singh."

As soon as the body is burned, the relatives return home. If a widow has been left, instead of words of comfort being spoken, she is assailed with abuse. She has at once to take off every article of jewellery, and for the rest of her life wear only white clothes. She is reminded that it is because of gross sins committed in a previous life that this great evil has come upon her, and she who ought to receive kindness and sympathy is made the drudge of the family. Certainly no class of women on earth are more miserable than Hindu widows. This, again, is the direct result of the teaching of books that the people believe have been given by the gods to teach men how they should live.

In some cases for three, in some for thirty days, the members of a family in which a death has occurred are unclean. No one eats with them, and they do not put on their usual dress. At the end of the days of mourning a great feast is made and religious ceremonies performed, the object of which is to secure the entrance of the spirit of the deceased into the company of the blessed in heaven. I have heard of funeral ceremonies in which ten thousand pounds were spent in religious ceremonies and gifts to Brāhmans and beggars, as a means of securing the well-being of some departed relative in the spirit world. When these ceremonies are concluded, there is no sign of mourning worn by the relatives.

CHAPTER XIII.

BAZAAR PREACHING.

Now that I have tried to give some idea of the city of Calcutta and its people, and also of their religion, I turn with pleasure to speak of the work in which the missionaries are engaged there. Of course, whatever may be the method of work, the aim is the same in all, viz., to lead the people to know that God who made them, loves them with a Father's love, and that Jesus came to show and Himself to be the way by which men might return to Him. But in trying to reach the minds and hearts of people such as the Hindus, we do not confine ourselves to any one form. I wish to say a little about several of these plans. In this chapter I shall speak of what is known as bazaar preaching.

The word "bazaar"—which, by the way, has been borrowed from India—suggests to people's minds in England a very different thing from the reality in India. A bazaar in England is often a very beautiful and attractive place. A town hall, schoolroom, or tent is gaily decorated, and stalls are arranged like a continental street, or Old English village. Young ladies dressed in most bewitching costumes make themselves as attractive as possible, as they try to sell the pretty and useful articles that willing hearts, inventive minds, and clever fingers have made. Few people have attended these bazaars without enjoying themselves, and almost wishing that they would continue for a lengthened period.

But in India the bazaar is a very different affair altogether. It means simply a collection of shops. Sometimes it may be a market hall, or something approaching it in some respects; sometimes it may simply be a street in which there are a number of shops. In Calcutta we have the China Bazaar, a narrow street where there are shops on both sides, in which clothing, dress goods, millinery, Chinese and Japanese curios, wines, beer and provisions, and a host of other things, can be purchased. Then we have the Bara Bazaar (the Big Bazaar), also a street, with shops on the upper as well as the lower flats, where piece goods from Yorkshire and Lancashire are sold wholesale, and also the silks, shawls, &c., that India produces; here are also on sale indigo, lac, and other Indian products. Then we have bazaars where meat, fish, fruit, and vegetables are exposed for sale. In fact, the word bazaar in India is used to describe the business part of a town; and bazaar preaching is, preaching in the public thoroughfares of a city where the great masses of the people are to be found.

This work is done in the cool hours of the morning or evening, either in the open air by the roadside, or in chapels that stand amongst a row of shops. The chapel in which I preached several times a week for years was a very simple structure indeed. It was built of mud, with mat doors, and would seat about a hundred and forty people; but sometimes it was

A NATIVE SHOP IN THE BAZAAR.

packed quite full, with crowds standing round the doors, which, as it was built at a corner, faced two streets. The seats are of the roughest description, and it is lighted by the commonest paraffin lamps. It was feared that if a more costly building were placed there, the people would not enter; but as it looks very much like the shops that are alongside, there is no danger of its being too beautiful.

Our audiences were of a most mixed character. There would be coolies, or labourers, waiting about to be hired to carry goods; young men and old returning from their work in the shops and offices in the city; and, as it stood near to the colleges, a goodly number of students who were having a little rest after class before their evening work commenced. There were men of high and low caste, Hindus and Mussulmāns; in fact, we had all sorts and conditions of men present; but no women—they would not think it right to come into a chapel where men were gathered together. When we were preaching in the open air, the women would generally walk outside the crowd, however curious they might be to know what the Englishman was saying to the people. This is one of the worst evils of Hinduism, that the women, if not confined in the Zenāna Khannahs, or women's apartments of the house, are afraid to be seen standing amongst a number of men in the streets, though it might be a crowd gathered round a missionary preaching.

English people make great mistakes as they think of the dress and appearance of missionaries at the present day at work in India. In pictures we appear dressed in a black dress-coat, a silk hat, and other things just as at home. But this is very far from the truth. In the mornings, during the greater part of the year, we wear white coats, white trousers, and a thick pith or cork helmet similar to those worn by the soldiers. In the evening the white coat is generally exchanged for an alpaca one. I fancy new-comers in India would be rather astonished as for the first time they saw a missionary going to his work. Seated on a tricycle, with white clothes and a drab helmet, with coloured spectacles to save himself from headache, and a great white umbrella in his hand;—this is a more truthful picture of his appearance now-a-days than the old ones I have just referred to. We try to dress in a way more suited to the climate than the old-fashioned style was.

On arriving at the place for preaching, the first thing to be done is to gather a congregation; for of course in the bazaar there is no settled audience such as that awaiting a minister on a Sunday morning in his church. The first thing we do is to read a few verses of Scripture, or what is better, if we have any one present able to do it, to sing a few verses of a Bengali hymn. The Bengalis are very fond of music, and a few verses of a hymn will collect a congregation far more quickly than anything else. If, however, we cannot manage this, we begin to read, or if one or two people are standing by, enter into conversation with them. The curiosity of the people is soon aroused as they see an Englishman and a Bengali in conversation. In the chapels, as soon as the lamps are lighted, a few people drop in, and before a chapter of Scripture has been read a fair number are ready to hear the preacher.

A great change has been made of late years in the style of preaching as it is carried on in the bazaars. When I first began to go out with the Bengali preachers I noticed that they scarcely said a word about Jesus and His teaching; they spent all their time in pointing out the evils and follies of heathen faith and practice, and their hearers would heartily laugh with them as they ridiculed many of their doings; but when it was evident that the preacher was going to speak of Christianity, the congregation would not hear them. Now, however, this has quite gone out of fashion—and a good thing too. The people have heard so much against idolatry, and education has exerted such great influence, that this is not necessary. In fact, often when I have been preaching of the love of Christ, if a man rose to defend Hinduism or to say he could not see any difference between Krishna and Christ, a Hindu better informed would say, "Do not you trouble to answer this poor ignorant man, I will do it for you;" and there would be seen the educated Hindu pointing out to his brethren the evils of the religion of their fathers. Now-a-days we often preach to Hindus very much in the same way as we preach to those in England who are not Christians.

Of course our services are not so orderly and quiet as are those in our churches at home. Some of the people sit for hours together to listen; others come and go, remaining for a few minutes only; some stand at the door, afraid to sit down lest it should be thought that they were about to become Christians. And often we are interrupted by men asking questions, or objecting to statements that we have made.

But this has become far less frequent of late, because it is known that when the address is concluded the people will be asked to talk about what has been said. Often I have sat for hours talking on religious subjects after the preaching was over. These "after meetings" are often of greater benefit than the address, because we learn how far the people have understood what we have said. For when a missionary has learned the Bengali language as it is spoken, his difficulties are not by any means over, as he learns when he attempts to impart Christian teaching; because he finds their religious words have a heathen association. Take *e.g.* the word "sin." If I preach to the people "Pāp kario nā" ("Do not sin"), this means to a Bengali, "Do not break your caste rules, do not become a Christian;" because "pāp" (sin) with him is not a violation of God's law of righteousness, but a violation of caste rules. When, therefore, we talk with the Hindus after preaching, we are able to see how far our words have been understood.

In former years it was a very common thing for some clever man who did not wish his friends to listen to the preacher, to raise some question for discussion in which he might show off his own knowledge and the ignorance of the preacher. He would try to lead the conversation away from Christianity to some such question as the origin of evil; asking, "Who made sin?" But now we never have anything of the kind. It is of immense importance that a missionary should not only know his Bible well, but also the Hindu sacred books, so that he may let the people see that when he says Christianity is better than Hinduism he knows what he is talking about; and further, he may often find in their books teaching of the highest importance which the people do not follow.

I have been associated with a good number of Bengali Christians in our preaching work, and have often been delighted to listen to their earnest and interesting addresses. When they preach they use illustrations largely, as these are easily understood and remembered. There was one man who often accompanied me in my work, who had the power of talking for hours together. But often his addresses were capital. Trying to show the people the goodness of God in providing for man's salvation, he said: "What would you think of our great queen if she came to your poor houses dressed as a Bengali in order that she might tell you how great her love for you was. Would you not clean the house, offer her your best seat, and give her all the good things that you could get for her? God has done this. He has come in Jesus Christ in the form of man. He wants to enter your homes, and dwell in your hearts; will you not receive and welcome Him who is the King of kings?" On another occasion he said: "What would you think of our queen if she went into a hospital where there were all kinds of sick people, that she might make them well—if she touched the eyes of the blind and gave them sight; made the dumb speak, and the leper clean; and when she saw some poor people weeping because their friend had died, weep with them, and then give life to the dead man? God has done this, and He is able and willing to make every one of you well now, and prepare you to appear before His throne." I think I have heard as good addresses in Bengali by men who were born in heathen homes as ever I heard in English churches.

It was very cheering, in going to this chapel week after week, to see the faces of people who came as regularly as they could, and, when asked why they came, to hear them say, "We have no other means of getting light from God. We come because the preaching does us good." Many of these people remain Hindus in name, because they have not courage to leave their homes, parents, friends—which they would have to do were they to be baptized and join the Christian Church. I have no doubt whatever that many of those I met at Bow Bazaar, if not in, were within a single step of Christ's Kingdom.

As I write, scenes rise up to memory that have been forgotten for years. One evening I noticed a young man who was most attentive throughout the service. When it was over, he came up to me, and in a most excited manner said, "Is it all true that you have been saying to-night, sir? Is it true that God forgives sin, and that He enables His children to know that they are forgiven?" I had been speaking from the words, "He that believeth on the Son hath everlasting life," and had said that the Christian had the assurance from God that his sins were forgiven. This youth went on to say, "I have of late been oppressed with the evil of my life, and the weight of my sins crushes me. During the last week I have twice attempted to kill myself. Although I have tried all Hindu ways of finding peace, my heart is sorely troubled. Can you give me hope?" I told him of Jesus and His work; and as he listened, the look of joy that lighted up his face was a blessed sight. I saw him often afterwards, and he always seemed happy and cheerful.

Often the students from the colleges came—sometimes to have a little fun at our expense. Occasionally their interest was excited, so that many came to visit me, and to attend Bible classes that I held at my house. From the youths we met at this chapel some of our best converts have been received.

I dare say people in England wonder how it is that far more of the Hindus who see the folly of Hinduism and the beauty of Christianity do not profess themselves to be Christians. It is simply because it necessitates their leaving home, parents, riches—everything, in fact, that is dear to them in this world. Whilst it is true that a few of the Christians in Bengal may be better off as Christians than they were as Hindus, of nearly all it may be said that for Christ's sake they have "left all." As Hindus, they would share the accommodation of the family house; as Christians, they must leave it. As Hindus, they would be loved and cared for by the members of their family; as Christians, they are as outcasts. As Hindus, they would find friends to help them on in life; as Christians, they find strong combinations against them. It is impossible for people who have not seen it to know the bitter hatred that is felt in Hindu homes for one who, before his baptism, was intensely loved, when he leaves his father's religion and becomes a Christian. Men who know all they have to suffer, rather wonder that so many should have courage to take the step that cuts them off from home and all its pleasures.

As our chapels are open to all comers, it sometimes happens that, as in political meetings in England, "rude men of the baser sort" come in to disturb our meetings; but not more than once or twice can I remember being seriously interfered with. Generally, by the exercise of a little patience and good temper, these disturbances are ended, and the influence of the better part of the audience soon leads to the discontinuance of the annoyance. Of course, in conversation, one had to listen to a good deal that was unpleasant, as men well read in infidel books, sent out from England, spoke against Christ and Christians; but these occasions were not frequent: and as I knew how we were sometimes compelled to shock the prejudices of some as we spoke of the evil doings of beings they worshipped as gods, I tried patiently to listen to their objections against Christianity. Looking back now over many years' experience of this work, I am simply astonished at the good temper of the Hindu congregations, and at the very attentive and respectful hearing they gave as we tried to lead them into the light. It is not pleasant to hear that all one's cherished faiths are groundless, and that one's religious opinions are founded on error; but this to a large extent is what the Hindu has to experience as we preach the gospel to him. As we speak of the excellence of Christ, by implication, if not in express terms, we condemn those who have occupied the place in their hearts that we wish Him to possess.

SCENE ON BANKS OF THE HUGLI.

CHAPTER XIV.

LIFE ON THE RIVERS.

ALTHOUGH Calcutta is a large city, it is not the whole of Bengal. There are great masses of people living in the country districts whom the missionary wishes to reach, and to whom he must go, as they cannot come to him. During the cold season, when travelling is safe, it is the practice of some missionaries to go out for weeks together, travelling from village to village and from town to town. By this means they have an opportunity of speaking to multitudes who otherwise would never hear the gospel. Bengal being well supplied with rivers as well as roads, there are two ways of reaching these country districts—by boat, or by road. In this chapter I shall speak of boat work.

As the rivers have been for many years the chief highway for travellers in certain parts of the country, very comfortable passenger-boats are always on hire. Those usually employed by Europeans and the respectable Bengalis are called Budgrows—flat-bottomed boats that will run up shallow streams, having one or two comfortable cabins. These rooms vary in size from, say, 8 feet by 4 to 12 feet by 8. The boats are hired at a certain charge per day: of this sum part goes to the owners of the boat and part to the men who row. The number of boatmen varies according to the size of the boat, some needing about four, others seven or eight. As there are no hotels *en route*, the boat serves for home by day and night; and as there are no shops in the villages where European food can be purchased, a good supply of the necessaries of life have to be taken in before starting. After a lesson I once learned, I was always most careful to see that the paraffin oil-can was *not* put

A BUDGEROW.

in the same box with bread, potatoes, &c.; for the cork coming out soon after we started, I had the pleasure of eating food and drinking tea with the flavour of this oil. Some people may like it, but I confess I do not. As, however, there was no chance of replenishing my stock of provisions for a fortnight, I had to be content with this highly flavoured food; and I scarcely ever see a paraffin lamp without this experience being brought vividly to mind.

Before starting on a journey, the first thing is to hire a boat. This is sometimes rather a tedious affair. At the landing-stage where the boats are moored, as soon as the boatmen see you, there is a rush to drag you on board. When the questions, "Where are you going?" and "How long are you to be away?" are answered, and the charge of the boat per day asked, all sorts of reasons are assigned for the fact that it cannot possibly be had for less than about double the price you are disposed to pay. Their books are brought out, in which it is shown that some Bengali gentleman had paid them the sum they demand; probably that agreement was written in their book by a clerk for about 3d., with the object of leading ignorant people to imagine that this was the correct price. After a lot of talk on both sides, they gradually come down to a trifle more than the first sum you named. When the charge is settled, an agreement, duly stamped, is drawn up, and a "baina," *i.e.* a small sum in advance, is given. As a rule, this settling of a bargain by a "baina" is considered binding. Once only did a boatman leave me in a difficulty by taking a better offer after he had agreed to let me have his boat. I could have prosecuted him for this, but it was not worth the trouble. Before starting, however, about half the sum to be paid for the journey has to be given, as a considerable amount has to be left by the boatmen with the owner of the boat, lest they should sail to some distant place and never return.

This reminds me of the universal custom that prevails with work-people when dealing with Europeans: they seldom or never commence any work until they have received a good part of the payment in advance. We should imagine that it is the native workman who should give the employer some guarantee of his completing his agreement. But the Bengali custom is quite the reverse of this. Possibly in years gone by unscrupulous Europeans have given work to Bengalis and then refused to pay them. Whatever the origin of the practice may be, it is scarcely possible to get a workman to move a finger until partial payment for his work has been received. To such an extent is this carried in some of the Calcutta workshops, that men draw money in advance for work that will take them six months at least to clear off. The masters say it is the best way they have of keeping their work-people together; otherwise when a firm is very busy, and are willing to pay a higher rate of wages, the people from other workshops would go to them: but being in debt, they are compelled to work on under their old employers. It certainly seems strange that when a bricklayer or carpenter comes to do any-work in a house, it is necessary to give him money, ostensibly for the purchase of materials, when his name and residence are unknown. Occasionally, but not frequently, they abscond with the prize, and laugh as they think they "have spoiled the Egyptians."

In starting for the rivers to the eastward of Calcutta, which have a dense population on their banks, our way for nearly a couple of days is through the Sunderbans of Bengal. The Sunderbans simply means a forest of sunder trees, a malarious district scarcely above the sea level, that is a perfect network of canals and rivers. Though I have passed through many times, I feel as much a stranger and in need of a guide there now, as the first time I went. There are no land-marks; each place looks like every other. After travelling for twelve hours, so far as the scenery is concerned it seems as if we had scarcely moved. Not many years ago this whole district, about two hundred miles long by fifty broad, was uninhabitable jungle. It is land that has gradually been formed by the immense quantities of mud that the Ganges, with its many mouths, has carried down from the fertile plains. In this rich soil trees have sprung up and decayed, until gradually the land has risen above the level of the water. To render the fields safe in times of unusally high floods, mud banks have been constructed.

These forests supply Calcutta with fuel. A little coal is used in European houses, but most of the cooking is done with wood fires. It is a sad life the wood-cutters live, owing to the prevalence of fever and the attacks of tigers. Often I have seen some of these poor people running to the nearest temple of Kāli to make a sacrifice to secure her protection for themselves and friends, and have heard stories of how these poor people, on their way to and from the idol, have been carried off by the tigers against whose attacks they were seeking protection.

As the forests are cleared the land is cultivated. At first, however, the crops are very small; but, fortunately for the landowners, there are tribes in India who are more averse to paying rent than any of the leaders of the No-Rent party in Ireland. These are the Santalis, one of the many tribes who inhabited India before the Hindus came there. Knowing that for three years they can "squat" in these newly-cleared fields rent-free, they come with their families and put up miserable huts, that will hang together for about the time they are required; and then they dig the ground, and sow their rice. For the first year they are almost at starvation point; but the second and third crops are much better. At the end of the third year they have the option of remaining at a low rental or clearing off. Strange to say, almost to a man they prefer to "move on to pastures new," rather than pay anything. They seem to have a settled conviction that the land is theirs, and that they ought not to recognize another's right to it by paying rent.

As we sail along these canals, we come here and there to the virgin forest; but generally on the sides of the canals by which we go, the land is under cultivation. It will greatly reduce the death-rate in Calcutta when the whole of this vast tract is tilled, as the east wind, which is said to be "good for neither man nor beast," is productive of malarious fever in Bengal, coming over this marshy district.

It is a most interesting sight as we glide along these rivers to see the many shapes and sizes of boats that are coming to the capital, laden with all the varied products of Eastern Bengal. Some immense boats are bearing jute, that will soon be on its way to Dundee to be made up into clothing, or carried to France to be mixed with silk for ladies' dresses. Some come with rice, which is to be shipped to feed the coolies who have been taken to work in the sugar-cane fields of the Mauritius and the West India

Islands. Some, nearly full of water, carry fish alive for the fish-eating Hindus; others have large cages in the water on either side, so that the fish are really living when they reach the markets. In a week or two these boats return heavily laden with the manufactures from the Lancashire looms. I do not know anything that gives one so good an idea of the greatness of the trade of India as a sail through the Sunderbans, and meeting all these heavily laden boats, carrying their rich freights to the one centre.

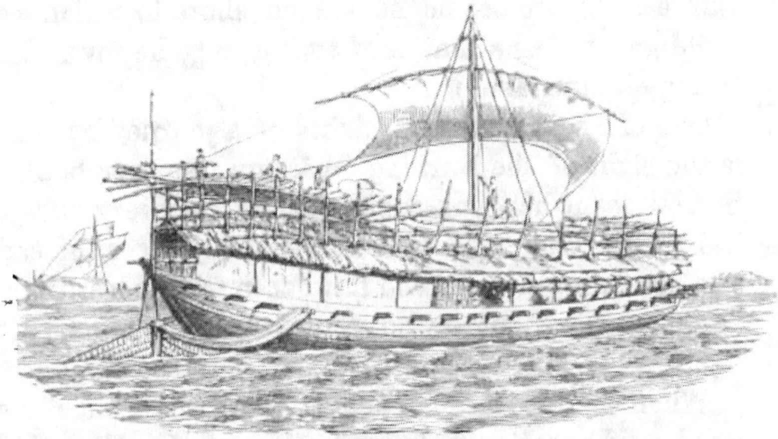

A CARGO-BOAT.

These canals are filled with salt water, and are not beyond the effect of the tide; and as the passenger and cargo boats are very heavy, and the currents swift, the men cannot possibly row against the stream. When, therefore, the tide is against us, we have either to wait for the turn, or to be towed by the boatmen. Towing is a slow, tedious process, as they seldom travel faster than about two miles an hour. And so great is their dread of tigers and ghosts, that the boatmen will not tow at night in most parts of the district.

As the streams wind about a great deal, here and there straight canals have been made to shorten the passage; as, however, these very soon get silted up, it frequently happens that one gets stuck fast in the middle, and has to wait about six hours for the water to rise. As the water runs out, and the mud banks and bottom of the stream are exposed to the terrific heat of the sun, and as there are hundreds of boats all close by, the stench is almost insufferable. I have a most lively recollection of hours spent under these circumstances. There are no houses on shore to which we could go; it was a matter of trying to be happy under trying circumstances.

One of the unpleasant sights of a journey by boat is the sight of the Burning Ghāts on the river banks. Sometimes it happens that near almost every village the fire is seen, and it tells, in many cases, of sad and sorrowing hearts, who have seen for the last time, as they believe, those who were dear to them as life itself.

When sailing through the Sunderbans, I once saw a splendid regatta. In former years, pirates abounded on the rivers; men professedly fishermen, were really robbers and murderers. For their work they had very long boats, in which twenty-four men could paddle. The descendants of these men are fishermen, and build their boats after the same pattern as those that were used for a far worse purpose. I have heard that even now, when an opportunity occurs, the people are not over-scrupulous. Their boats are very swift and the rowers numerous, so that they can overtake any ordinary boat, and destroy its crew. And as there are few to interrupt their proceedings, it is a wonder that more murders are not committed in these parts. On the day in question prizes were offered, and about a dozen long and well-manned boats started. I certainly never saw boats fly through the water as these did. Their bows were literally lifted out of the water with each stroke, and when a boat fouled another, the language and gesticulations were such as almost made one's hair to stand on end. I have heard London cab and omnibus men use uncomplimentary expressions, but, for strength of language in anger, I think the boatmen of Bengal beat all. Fortunately their anger expends itself in words; for certainly if the same degree of fire were kindled amongst Englishmen, torrents of blood, rather than of mere eloquence, would flow to quench it. Often in the streets when friends and neighbours fall out, they "chide," but seldom fight. Their war of words goes on for hours together; and if new expletives are not forthcoming, and further abuse cannot be given, the offensive terms are repeated hundreds of times, under the impression, I suppose, that there is power in numbers. A quarrel between a couple of women of the lower orders exhibits as good dramatic powers as ever were exhibited by ranting actors on a tragedy stage.

To any one going on a boat journey at the time of the great Mohammedan feast called the Rāmzān—which continues for twenty-eight days, during which the men eat once only in the day—I should give Punch's advice to those about to marry, and say "Don't." Ignorant though these men may be, they are generally most scrupulous about this fast; and as the month progresses they become so weak and, consequently, bad tempered, that it is not at all pleasant to sail with them. At other times they are generally a decent set of fellows. This boat work is almost exclusively in the hands of the people who come from the far east of the province.

In travelling through this district one sees some interesting sights. Once I sat and watched men fishing with otters. They sit on board a boat, holding a chain attached to the animals, which are hired month by month from the trainers, and throw them into the water. In a few minutes the otter is seen with a big fish in its mouth, when it is immediately dragged on board, and sent to fetch another. These poor animals have rather a hard time of it—catching the fish, but allowed to eat only about enough to keep them alive, lest they should grow lazy.

On the journey through the Sunderbans there are not many people; a few scattered villages only, so that our work does not really commence until we reach the rivers beyond. There we have work enough to satisfy the most active. Part of most days is spent in travelling, but in the morning and evening we have opportunities of talking to the heart's content.

In the morning, work is quiet and unexciting. The missionary visits the villages near the banks, or the houses of the gentry. In the cottages of the labourers there is no room for strangers; and they do not care for a Christian to sit in the room where their food is being prepared: but in the larger Hindu houses there is the courtyard with its verandahs, and as we enter these a number of the people from the cottages do not fear to flock round to hear what we have to say.

I have been delighted with the way in which at once we are able to commence a conversation on religious matters with the Hindus. It is expected of us. After asking the name of the gentleman in whose house we are sitting, and telling him our own and the business we follow, they look for a religious talk. There is no need to lead the conversation up to it. And as "the Hindu's house is *not* his castle," but is open to all comers, we have capital opportunities in these places of telling the people the message of God's love we have brought to them. I fear that some of our anti-tobacco friends would be rather scandalized were they to see some of these gatherings; for as we sit and talk to the people in this friendly style, their pipes are brought out, and pass from hand to hand—those belonging to one caste of course being allowed to use only the pipe of men of the same caste. We should certainly not have a lengthened conversation if we were to attempt to prohibit the use of the pipe.

Perhaps here a word may be said about the use of tobacco in India. It is almost universally "drunk" by the Hindus—for that is the idiom; they always speak of "drinking" the smoke. Just as in parts of Kent you see a small patch of ground most carefully tended where the hop vines grow; so in a corner of most of the farms in Bengal you see a little tobacco growing. It is not considered respectable for women to smoke, though a good number of the fair sex do indulge in the use of it; but I do not think I have met with half a dozen men who do not smoke. Boys never smoke in the presence of their fathers, nor students in the company of their tutors. I have noticed frequently that when even grey-headed men wish to smoke, if any one is present who has been in the position of tutor or master to them, they quietly go aside, as it is thought disrespectful to smoke in the presence of a superior. With the Bengali, smoking is a business that absorbs his whole attention for the time. The ordinary pipe, commonly known as the Hubble-Bubble, from the noise made by it when in use, is a cocoa-nut shell filled with water. To this are fixed two tubes, the longer of which goes to the bottom of the water; and on the other end a clay cup is attached, into which the tobacco and

A BENGALI PIPE.

burning charcoal are put: the other, which goes inside the nut above the water, is the one that is put into the mouth. This cumbersome instrument is held in the hand, often indeed with the two hands, when being used. The tobacco, mixed with molasses, is so damp that it will not burn unless some more combustible material is put with it. Hence charcoal is used for this purpose. As the air is drawn through the water a gurgling sound is heard, which has led to the expressive name of Hubble-Bubble being given to it. A few whiffs are taken, and the pipe is handed on to the next eager watcher; and whilst we talk on the most important questions, the friendly pipe goes round, and the people remain to hear what we may have to say.

Sometimes we sit under the shade of a tree in the middle of the village, and there talk with the villagers; or enter the school, where we are always welcomed, and asked to examine the pupils and record our impressions of the virtues of the teachers in the visitors' book for the gaze of the school inspector on his next visit. After a talk with the boys, a congregation of anxious parents having gathered round the door, we go to them and tell them of the Great Teacher and Saviour of men. Generally the days spent in the villages are most busy, as the people are anxious to hear all we have to say, and generally they talk freely with us on religious questions.

But it is in the afternoons that our heavy work comes. In the great majority of the villages there is not a single shop. How then are the people to buy their necessaries and sell their grain and manufactures? Their wants in this respect are met by weekly or bi-weekly Hāts, or markets. Within a distance of about three or four miles from every village, these hāts are to be found: some of which may not be attended by more than five hundred, some of them drawing at least ten thousand people together. We arrange our journey so as to attend a market every day. I went through a market-place one morning, and it looked quite a desert. It was an open space, well shaded by immense trees. There were a few sheds, open on all sides, having a roof of palm leaves; but no counters or furniture of any description. But by twelve o'clock it was the busiest hive one could imagine. With the tide, boats of every description came rushing in; some were trees hollowed out, only large enough to carry a couple of people; others bearing a freight of over a hundred people, with all their goods for sale. I reckoned that there were more than ten thousand people on the ground. And a busy time we had, selling Bibles,

A VILLAGE MARKET-PLACE.

giving small tracts, preaching to immense congregations, talking with individuals, until the sun went down. A more interesting and exciting day's work I never had; nor shall I ever forget the sight of these people hurrying into their boats as the sun was sinking and the moon rising. More fascinating and interesting work than this, when one is familiar with the language of the people and has any "enthusiasm of humanity," it would be hard to imagine. The people are very ignorant, it is true; but their ignorance, and earnestness in religious matters, although they are "very superstitious," as were the Athenians of old, appeals the more to one's sympathies, and calls forth all one's energies to put the truth of God in a form at once intelligible and acceptable to them.

A BENGALI COUNTRY SCENE.

CHAPTER XV.

LIFE IN TENT.

India, though in many districts well supplied with rivers, is not destitute of good roads, on the sides of which there are thousands of large towns and villages where no Christian teacher is living. Many of these are too far distant from the river banks to be visited from the boats; and, moreover, the hiring of boats is rather an expensive matter. Where good roads exist, a far cheaper and, for some reasons, a better way of working is by the use of tents. In England it is easy to find accommodation in hotels and boarding-houses; but in India, outside of the towns where Europeans live in some numbers, these very convenient places do not exist. In some districts the Government Dāk Bungalows are available; but they are seldom used by missionaries, as they do not happen to be in places where he wishes to go. Of course when they are convenient for his work, it is a great boon to occupy them.

Tenting in some parts of the country is as enjoyable a life as one could imagine. I have lived under canvas in the North-West Provinces, and enjoyed it immensely. There, at convenient distances, say about ten miles apart, along the main roads the Government has planted orchards large enough to shelter the camp of a regiment of soldiers when on march. Under the shade of the beautiful mango trees, one can live all day, having one's meals outside the tent, using it simply as a bed and dressing-room; for the people seldom look on as we eat, as this is quite contrary to Hindu etiquette. They do not like to be looked at in similar circumstances, nor do they trouble others with their presence when food is about. Moreover, the air is so dry in the cold season, that it would be safe to sleep under the trees without a tent, with a good blanket wrapped round the body. But tenting in Lower Bengal has its drawbacks. There are no orchards in which to pitch a tent; and the air is saturated with moisure, so that at night the inner tent walls are completely wet through. In the districts around Calcutta in the tent it is exceedingly hot by day, because no shady places can be found, and just as cold at night. Again, the roads in the North-West Provinces of India are capitally kept; whereas in Bengal they are generally rough and dusty. Except in the city of Calcutta, they are made of burnt bricks, so that when the wind blows dense clouds of dust arise almost enough to blind one; whilst the "cutcha" or mud roads have ruts nearly a foot deep, so that one's boxes get terribly shaken as they are carried along in the springless hackeries or bullock-carts. As long as your cart keeps in the ruts it is all very well; but when you have to get out of the way of a cart coming in the opposite direction, it is not a very pleasant matter. We generally walk from one camping ground to the next, a march of about ten miles.

When tenting is done regardless of cost, it is very enjoyable; but when missionaries travel, as they do, in an economical manner, there are a few drawbacks

A BULLOCK-CART.

to it. Civil officers, when "in the district," as it is called, have two tents; the day before the march one of these is taken down and carried to the next stage and pitched. After a good breakfast the gentleman mounts his horse, inspects the villages with their police offices, &c., and when he reaches his new lodging-place his tent and dinner are awaiting him. But we have to do things in a much less luxurious style. Rising before daybreak, we get a hurried cup of tea and slice of toast, pack up our bedding, &c., and then work hard for an hour or more in taking down the tent and packing it on the bullock-carts; and, when all is ready, start for a ten-mile walk. Reaching the village, and having found the best spot for our tent, we have to wait for a couple of hours or more for the slow-moving carts to come up. When the carts are unloaded, there comes an hour's hard work in pitching the tent and getting things into order. By about one or two o'clock, if no accident has happened, breakfast is ready, not a moment before we are both tired and hungry. If a cart breaks down—by no means an unusual thing—there is a still longer trial of patience. But, "as all things come to him who waits," breakfast-time comes at last, and a good meal and a little rest restore one to good humour.

Sometimes, when weary with walking, I have been tempted to hire an Ekka. This is a purely native vehicle for *one* person, as its name implies. It has no springs, and when a pony goes at full gallop with this machine over a rough road—and most of the Bengali roads are very rough—the shaking is about as much as can be got out of any mode of travelling that I have tried. These ekkas are sometimes used as mail-carts.

The cleverness of the Indian servants is well manifested when out tenting. They seem to be in their element cooking amid difficulties. I have been astonished, and pleased too, to see how quickly and well, after a long march, with no proper place to cook in, they put a really good meal upon the table. On a long march, when away from home for nearly a month, I have never had to complain of the cooking of the food; but everything was as well and cleanly done as it would have been at home. It may be, of course, that the fresh air and healthy exercise supplied us with the best known sauce—hunger.

AN EKKA.

Our work in the villages near the tent is carried on very much in the same way as when we go by boat; there is, however, this additional benefit, that, remaining in the same place for three or four days, our presence is known in the district, and people come to talk with us in a quiet and confidential manner. Seated in the shade of the tent, as they come in numbers, we can go on teaching all the day. In the mornings we visit the villages, in the afternoon the hāts; but the time that is lost in moving from place to place when travelling by boat is available for teaching at our tent-door. At first the people are a little shy; but when we have visited the same villages year after year all their fears are dispelled, and they keep us well employed from morning till night. After a three weeks' work of this kind one can appreciate the loving thoughtfulness of Jesus, when He said to His disciples on their return from a similar tour, "Come ye apart and rest awhile."

It must not be supposed that the Hindus are always glad to see us in their villages. At first they do not know who we are or what we want. It is not until they see we "seek not theirs but them," to do good and not harm, that they manifest joy at our presence. I remember once entering a village and asking a man to direct me to the house of the head-man, the recognized leader of the village community. Never having seen me before, and fearing that some evil might follow my visit, he took me along winding roads; and, after a quarter of an hour's walk, I found myself away from the village altogether. This is just an illustration of the Bengali character: he tried to prevent me from going to his own village, but he put me in the way for passing on to the next. I once saw a man with some furious animal in a bag. Inquiring what it was, I was told that it was a mad cat. This cat had been a source of great annoyance to the people in his village, but as the cat is especially sacred to the goddess Sasthi, the guardian of women and children, he dare not kill it, lest all the ladies and babies should suffer. He therefore caught the cat, put it in a bag, and carried it to the opposite side of the river. By this means the nuisance was got rid of so far as he was concerned, and Sasthi could not be angry, because he had done no injury to her pet.

Even tent-life has its drawbacks. Although the weather in the cold season is generally beautiful, occasionally it is the reverse. Though a tent is very comfortable when the wind is calm, it is not so nice in a storm. Sometimes we are awakened by the sound of wind, and there is a motion in the canvas that is anything but pleasant. If care is not taken at once to tighten the cords, the whole will come down like a pack of cards; and it is not at all pleasant to be out in the open with the rain pouring down upon your clothes, beds, and eatables. If the rain continues for long, the ground becomes so soft that the tent-pegs cannot be made to stick. From what I have seen of storms, I am decidedly of opinion that it is safer to be outside than inside a tent when a strong nor'-wester is blowing.

Going about from village to village, one sees some sights that are not customary in England. In some districts it is not at all uncommon to see a troop of big blacked-faced monkeys sitting chattering on the trees, or running about from shop to shop in the village market, helping themselves to the vegetables and fruit to supply their own and their children's wants. The people do not attempt to drive them away forcibly, as they are the representatives of Hanumān, the great leader of the monkeys, who proved of such great assistance to Rāma, the popular god. When their peculations become very extensive, the shopkeepers may try in a good-natured way to induce them to run away, but generally they are not disturbed. I once received rather too much attention from a number of these four-handed animals. Having with me a little dog that evidently had not been often in the presence of monkeys, and who expressed his surprise at their appearance in a manner that irritated them, about twenty of them made an attack upon the little terrier. I knew that, if once they caught him, he would be carried to a tree and there torn to pieces; and as I had nothing but an umbrella to defend myself with, the odds were rather against me for a time. I confess I was rather annoyed to see the villagers standing as mere spectators of the game, evidently wishing to see fair play, for not one of them raised a a finger to help me. With my open umbrella I managed to shelter the dog, whilst I "marched backwards" as quickly as possible until I was near enough to call to my companions for help. I have no wish for another encounter with monkeys.

Another strange sight is the Shār, or religious bullock. When a Hindu who worships Siva dies, it is a common thing for a bull to be branded with a trident, the emblem of Siva, and let loose to wander where it will, much in the same way as the scapegoat was set free in Israel. These bulls, being sacred, are allowed to roam through the rice fields and do what damage they wish to the crops, as no Hindu interferes with them. But there are Mussulmāns as well as Hindus, whose fields are not separated by hedges as in England. If the shār happens to get into one of these fields, woe betide him. He is beaten and stoned, and of late years many of them have been caught and removed to the cities, where they are put to the degrading work of dragging conservancy and other carts. The setting free of a bull, Siva's favourite animal, is supposed in some way to secure the happiness in heaven of the person on whose behalf it is done.

In the markets, one of the sights that a stranger would notice is the barbers plying their razors. The Hindus never shave themselves. Division of labour is carried to perfection in India. When, therefore, a man comes to market, he of course pays a visit to the barber, who has a lot of work to do for a pice, *i.e.* about one and a half farthings. He cuts a man's hair, shaves him on the face and under the arm-pits, cuts his finger and toe nails, and cleans his ears. Many of the people have their heads also partly shaved; but whenever the head is shaved, there is always a small tuft left, so that there may be something by which they can be dragged up to heaven. It is astonishing to see how religious notions rule all the affairs of life.

As the cold season is a busy time with the people in the fields, sometimes when we go out to work in the early morning we find the villages quite empty, the men being away at their work; if therefore we wish to reach them, we must follow. First we come in sight of a number at work engaged in making gur, or molasses, from which sugar is refined. Sugar-cane is cultivated, but it is mostly from the date palm that the juice is obtained. To get this juice, men climb the tree, and after cutting a notch through the bark, a tube is inserted, which conducts the sap into a jar fixed to receive it. In the evening these jars are collected, and the sap boiled until it becomes a hard, brown stuff, rather like toffy. The men have to keep the fires going all day long; but as the white man comes they leave their work for a few minutes, that they may listen to what he has to say. Sometimes, but very seldom, are they too much engrossed in their work to listen.

Then we come to a farmyard, where threshing of corn is going on. These threshing-floors are simply mud, and instead of steam threshing-machines, bullocks are driven round and round to tread out the corn. When the straw is threshed, it is winnowed in a very simple manner. One man takes up a little on

HARROWING.

a sort of tray, and lets it fall slowly to the ground, whilst another waves a tray up and down to blow away the chaff. The character of the threshing-floors accounts for the fact that the Indian wheat, which is now coming in such large quantities to England, is so full of mud. It would be impossible for the wheat to be clean when threshed on a mud floor.

Now we hear of a "Barawari," a religious festival got up by a number of villagers. In places where there happens to be no rich Hindu gentleman near, and no large Hindu house, a subscription is opened amongst the villagers, a temporary mat temple erected, an image ordered, a priest engaged, and a troup of singers or players brought, so that the people may have the pleasure of having a god worshipped in their neighbourhood, and of witnessing the performances of the professional players.

In another place we hear of a new shrine being established. We find that some one having been told that some one else had seen a spirit hovering over a tank, advantage is taken of the report to raise a good income from the simplicity and trustfulness of the people. A company of about thirty men is formed, about half of whom go from place to place, singing the merits of the shrine, and telling the people of the benefits that multitudes of sick people have received from visiting it. The others put up a mat temple at first, and a few brick ends covered with a sheet, for a god, and there wait to receive the gifts of the people. When I visited a place of this kind, I saw hundreds of people who had been induced to come in search of health, some having passed by good hospitals in order that they might be benefited by recourse to a place like this. The simplicity of the people of India in many respects is remarkable.

In fact, when out in the country districts, the missionary goes wherever he thinks it at all likely that he will gain a good audience or meet with a goodly number of people; and generally after a day's labour sleeps well, because "his something attempted and something done has earned a night's repose." His audience varies from units to thousands. His church is generally the open air, his pulpit a stool or the stump of a tree. There are none of the luxuries one sees in our comfortable and beautiful churches in England. He has not always the respectful attention that is accorded in Christian congregations. A noisy questioner may stop him in the midst of one of his orations with a question not very easy to answer. But he comes close to the people, who, as a rule, are willing to hear what he has to say, to whom his message has at least the shape of novelty. A very indifferent preacher in England, one who is charged with never saying anything new, certainly will not hear his Hindu congregation find this fault with him. His message is quite different from what Hinduism teaches; and, so far as I can remember, only once in the course of years was I prevented from saying what was in my heart to the people. On this occasion we had visited a festival which lasted three days; the first two days we did splendidly in selling Bibles and tracts, and in preaching. Going the third day, we saw an angry look on the faces of a few men, who were determined to put a stop to our work. Taking one quietly apart, I found that the priests had found the money spent on Bibles was so much loss to them. "Their craft was in danger," like that of the silversmiths at Ephesus, and we were given clearly to understand that we should not be allowed to preach. As I was the only Englishman within forty or fifty miles, and there was no effectual help to be had from the police, I thought it advisable under the circumstances to be quiet, and wait for happier times. For though ordinarily a law-respecting people, in moments of excitement the Bengalis are capable of violence.

CHAPTER XVI.

ALL ABOUT TIGERS.

WHEN missionaries and other travellers return from Africa, it is quite expected that they have something to say about lions; in fact, a book on Africa that did not mention them, would seem to come altogether below one's ideal. And as tigers occupy about the same position in India as lions do in Africa, one feels bound when writing about India to say something about them.

First, then, let it be known that tigers are not to be found everywhere. It is as difficult to meet with them in some parts of India as it would be in England. Tigers have a habit of getting away from civilization; they pass away from the presence of cultivation as some of the darker races of men disappear before the advancing white. To-day, for hundreds of miles together in India, no tigers are to be met with, though in years gone by they were there in numbers. As a matter of fact, most English people, after a long residence in India, have to confess that during all the years they lived there they never saw one except behind the bars of a cage. There are still many to be found, but it is necessary to go into tiger districts to see them.

And these districts are steadily diminishing. Some of the princes who wish to entertain British noblemen

A CRITICAL MOMENT.

visiting India for sport, or the officers of Government who are anxious to have "a pot at a tiger," enclose miles of territory that these wild beasts may live unmolested, or very soon they would become as scarce as badgers at home. The lands that for centuries have been uncultivated, as the population increases, become tilled; this gives the tigers notice to leave, and the Government offers a reward of ten shillings, to any who bring in a dead tiger to the police-stations. This encourages the people to try to get rid of them by means of guns, swords, and spears.

If Calcutta sportsmen wish to have sight of a tiger on "his native heath," or in his own royal forest, he must go about thirty or forty miles into the Sunderbans. It was there that I had my first and last view of a real Bengal tiger in his wild state. As the river on which I was travelling passed through the "forest primeval," and I knew that tigers were to be found there, I gave strict orders to my boatman to tell me if any royal visitor appeared. Just at dawn my cabin door was gently opened, and the welcome news came, "Bāgh hai, sahib," *i.e.* "There is a tiger here, sir!" Up I jumped, and as I stood on the deck of the boat I saw a beautifully striped skin which I hoped might soon be mine. The bank on which he stood was only about a dozen yards from my boat. I quietly slipped down for my rifle; but alas, when I returned, my visitor had disappeared. Now had I been venturesome as a few sportsmen are, I should have nimbly jumped ashore and challenged the tiger to single combat; but I confess I did not feel quite up to that. I have heard of one or two gentlemen in Calcutta who go into this very neighbourhood, and walk through the dense jungle in the hope of meeting a tiger, as this is the only way of reaching them in the Sunderbans; the woods are too thick to allow elephants to penetrate them. But it seems to me to be a foolhardy trick. Were the rifle to fail, it would only be the work of a moment for the tiger to strike his assailant dead with his paw, and drink his blood.

People make a great mistake about tigers, and lions too, when they imagine that they are brave and courageous animals. When one of these beasts is wounded it will attack its assailant, or if it has young cubs in charge it will shed its life-blood in defending them; but horses, cows, and even sheep will fight to defend their little ones. As a rule, a royal tiger will escape if it sees any way open; but if it can get away only by making one through its foes, it will then try this. Watch a cat chasing a mouse, and you see the tiger's tactics truthfully illustrated. Although we know that hundreds of people every year are killed and eaten by tigers, it is almost an unknown occurrence for one to attack a party of men; it is when one lags behind his companions and the tiger can pounce upon him and carry him off by stealth that he attempts this. Or if a man be sleeping in an open place, a tiger will seize him; but if two or three men keep together when travelling through a district known to be the haunt of these wild beasts, unless they meet with a tigress and cubs they are safe from attack.

In going down to Saugar Island to visit the great festival which I have already described, some of our number had a great fright. Wishing to go for a walk inland when our boat came to anchor "waiting for the turn of the tide," they wandered on, pleased with the beauties of the forest. But after a little time they were startled by hearing a loud roar which told them that some one was rather objecting to his territory being disturbed. As they had no firearms or other weapons, excepting those nature had given them, they thought the best thing they could do was to show that in one respect they were superior to the gentleman who disputed their right to wander in the woods. They could climb a tree; but the tiger could not. So up a tree they went, and there they remained from evening until daylight. They shook with cold and fear during the long hours of night; all in the boat grew anxious, until at last they came shouting to the river-side and narrated their experience as night watchmen.

So far as I am aware, excepting in the way mentioned above, no hunting of tigers goes on in the Sunderbans; but as the forests are cleared, and the land brought under cultivation, the area of these royal Bengals becomes considerably diminished, so that in a few years time the district will be free from them.

Stretching for hundreds of miles along the foot of the Himālayah Mountains is a belt of land varying in width from eight to twenty miles. This country is known as the Terai, and is perhaps as fertile as any land on the face of the earth. This has been uncultivated and uninhabited by man, because it is so intensely malarious. For most people a night spent in it would prove almost certain death. There, owing to the heat and moisture, nature has revelled in its productions. Immense trees spread their branches, and grass, known as tiger grass, grows to a height of twelve to fifteen feet. This is pre-eminently the home of tigers and other wild beasts. Gradually, however, this is being cultivated, and some of the finest tea-gardens in India are flourishing where only a few years ago was the densest jungle.

As the trees do not grow so closely together here as in the Sunderbans, elephants can be employed in hunting: and every year numbers of gentlemen go mounted on the backs of these huge creatures, where they are tolerably safe. Occasionally they have a narrow escape. A tiger wounded is a most desperate beast. It may make a rush up the side of the elephant in its attempt to reach its assailants; or it may seize the elephant by its trunk: and tame and controllable though this sagacious animal may usually be, to remain quiet with the claws and teeth of a tiger fastened to its trunk is more than most elephant natures can manage. Brought into such close quarters, if the hunter keep cool, a well-directed shot removes the cause of danger; but if the elephant become unmanageable, or, being new to the work, does not give heed to the mahout's guidance, the position of those on his back is most critical. As he rushes away, they stand a very good chance of having their heads smashed against the boughs of the trees. When hunting with elephants, a number of men on foot are employed to find out a tiger's hiding-place, and, if possible, to drive him in the direction of the sportsmen.

In the North-West Provinces of India is a far safer though perhaps less exciting method of tiger-hunting. When it is known that a tiger is within a few miles of a certain place, a machān is built in a tree where there is a little open space in front. A machān is a rude platform made with bamboos on the branches of a tree, on which the sportsman can sit with his rifle ready to hand. Sometimes a bullock is tied to a stake at a little distance from the machān so that a tiger may be attracted by his cry. After killing his prey and drinking his blood, he is satisfied for one night, and will probably remain near ready for the next day's feed. Early in the afternoon the sportsman takes his place in the tree, whilst about a hundred beaters commence their work. A number of these men start a couple of miles away, shouting and beating their tom-toms to drive Mr. Stripes towards the tree; others stand on either side leaving a good distance between them. These men watch the grass, and as they see it move they guess where the tiger is, although he does not show himself. By making a little noise, they drive him into the centre of the space enclosed by the beaters on the other side. Frightened by the approaching shouts of the men behind, he goes nearer and nearer to the fatal spot, and as the beaters on either side gradually approach each other, the animal is driven within shot. Often it happens that he makes a rush past the tree like a flash of lightning, so that the sportsman above has only a few seconds for his aim. Sometimes the beast escapes; but in a well-managed hunt the chances are decidedly against him. Occasionally, seeing himself hemmed in, the tiger attacks the beaters; but many a tiger is bagged without harm coming to any one. The ordinary pay of the beaters is an anna (1½d.) if there is no sport; or half as much more if the day's work is successful.

I once happened to come into a village where an officer of the Government was in camp, who had enjoyed good sport the previous day. I was interested in seeing the machān and the spot where the king of the forest had fallen. Wishing to see the tiger himself, I went to a village of basket-makers a mile or two distant. These are a low-caste people who do not refuse to eat flesh. Asking to be allowed to see the game, I was told that he was already disposed of; not a square inch of him remained. The villagers had enjoyed an unusual feed, and many of them were sleeping off its effects.

As I said above, once only did I *see* a tiger in his own proper domain; but I had the pleasure of hearing them for several nights in succession: and travelling as we were, I was quite satisfied with that. A Benares missionary, the Rev. D. Hutton, and myself were travelling to an out-station of the Benares Mission, the road to which, if it is worthy of the name, lay through a a jungle-district; one of the noted hunting-grounds of the North-West Provinces. After getting out of the cultivated into the wild, uninhabited parts, I confess the first night I felt a little interested in the fire outside our tent; and was most careful to see that it burnt brightly, even getting out of my warm bed to throw on a few logs of wood to warn off the roaring beasts. But seeing no harm came, one grew bolder; especially as at several places we found a small space with stockades of bamboos, in which to pitch our tent, and keep our camels and bullocks safe.

No doubt the tiger stories we heard from those who had been here before did not give us much comfort. The place was indicated on the march where one of our missionaries had seen a tiger and his wife deliberately marching towards him; but who, before they met, politely turned out of the road and went their way. Another spot was pointed out where this same gentleman had the pleasure of watching the interesting spectacle of a tiger chasing an antelope. A most marvellous story was told of another missionary who, tired of the slow march of the men who carried his tent, went on ahead quite alone. Seeing something move in the grass a little in front, he had just time to raise his rifle and fire. Being a good shot, the bullet entered the breast of the tiger as it was in the act of springing upon him. And it certainly did not add to our comfort to walk for miles tracking the footsteps in the sand of a pair of tigers or leopards.

Still, after a day's march the nervousness wore off, and we slept the sleep of the weary after our long marches, although again and again the roar of the beasts reached us in our tents. One of our camping-grounds I shall never forget. Its beauty is photographed upon my memory, and rises as distinct to view as though it were actually within sight. The spot where our tent was pitched was on a sloping lawn, with grass as soft as velvet, and as beautifully cut as if a patent lawn-mower had been over it. At this spot the river was shallow, so that cattle could ford it; and when we were there immense droves of cattle were led across on their way to the plains, where in the hot season there was good pasturage. On the opposite bank was a dense forest stretching for miles, the home of tigers and other large game. To the extreme right rose a rock 1,900 feet high, almost perpendicular to the water's edge. It was beautiful during the day; but as the full moon rose it gave an unearthly charm to the scene: and when about ten o'clock at night an eclipse came on, there was an

A DRAUGHT BULLOCK.

additional cause of interest. For as we sat watching the shadow grow, the herdsmen, gathered round their fires in the distance, set up the most terrible shouts to drive away the giant, lest the moon should be for ever lost. It was well worth all the weariness and discomforts of the journey to witness a sight such as this. On this journey I saw an immense number of bullocks that are used throughout the district to carry grain. As there are no roads, all the produce of the country is carried by these animals. Now that I am writing a chapter about tigers, I almost wish I had come into closer contact with them. There is always a pleasure in narrating an adventure; but as I had no idea when on the journey of doing anything of the kind, I was thankful that they kept at a respectful distance. I never went, in Don Quixote fashion, in search of an adventure, or India would have afforded a capital field. Once I confess I felt I was doing a rather unwise thing, and had a mild scare for my pains. At a little distance from a friend's house where I was staying, was a hill towards which a number of pilgrims were plodding their weary way. My host suggested we should make the ascent. There was a good beaten track, but this we despised, preferring rather to make our way up the steep sides through the jungle that covered it. After a time we came to a spot a little more open, with an overhanging rock. On examination we found that this was a leopard's or a bear's home, and that its owner had not long left it. As we were armed only with umbrellas, we were not at all sorry when we found ourselves on the beaten road, to which we strictly kept for the rest of the ascent.

CHAPTER XVII.

SCHOOL WORK.

IN addition to the evangelistic work, or preaching to the adults, a very important branch of Mission agency in India is that of teaching in schools and colleges. Most of the Missionary Societies have their "Institutions," as they are called, that are opened for the purpose of giving Christian education to boys and young men, almost exclusively in English. In most parts of the country there is a great desire to study English, and to appear in the University examinations, because of the higher social position and larger salaries that English-speaking natives can secure. Many of the poorer people, and of the lower castes, deny themselves of almost the necessaries of life in order that their sons may, by receiving a good education, obtain a better start in life than they enjoyed themselves.

Education of a high order can be secured at the Government schools and colleges; why then do the missionaries devote their time to this work? The answer to this question lies in the fact that India possesses one of the oldest systems of religion existing amongst men; and this religion retains a firm grasp of the faith and devotion of the people because it boasts of some of the oldest religious literature. As our missionaries preached Christ as the Saviour, the people asked, "When did Jesus appear?" On being told that he was born in Bethlehem some eighteen hundred years ago, they replied, "Your religion is a

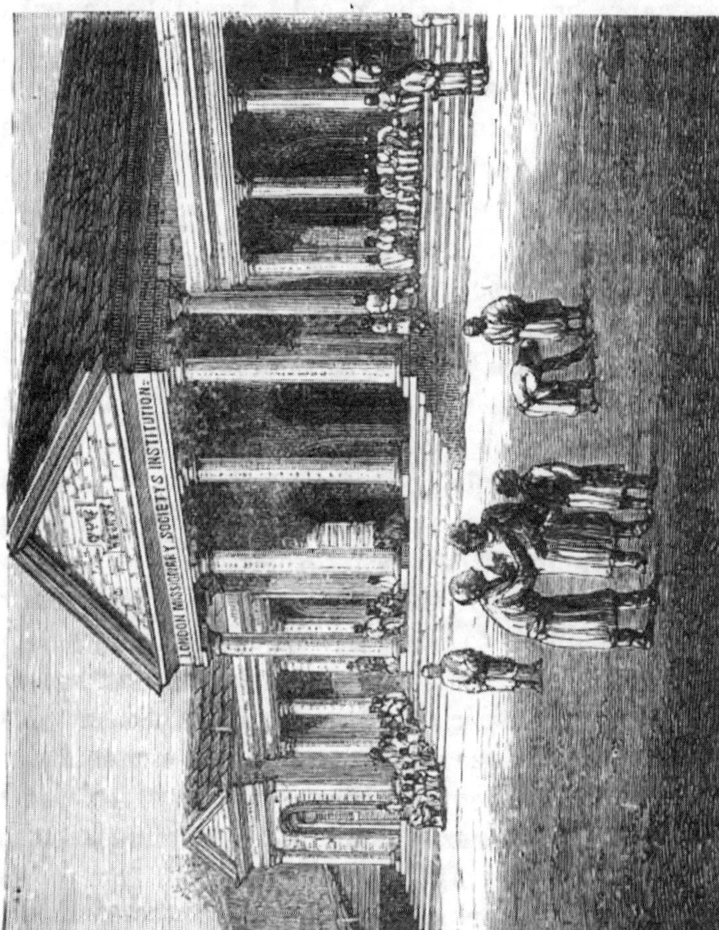

A MISSION SCHOOL.

thing of yesterday. Our books were written hundreds of thousands of years ago, and our religion, because of its age, must be a far better system that anything that was proclaimed so recently." The faith of the

Hindus in their sacred writings was unbounded; and about forty years ago, some of the ablest of the missionaries thought if this faith in the Divine origin of these books could be destroyed, they could then reasonably hope that the people would listen with unprejudiced minds to their statements respecting Christianity. The mind of India was like jungle-covered land: this jungle needed to be cut down before the soil could receive the good seed of the kingdom. The mind of India was wrapped in the grossest darkness: it was necessary for light to enter that they might be able to see and appreciate "the unsearchable riches of Christ."

With this object Christian schools were opened; and partly because the fees charged are lower than those of the Government schools, and partly because it is known that as a rule the missionaries are kinder to their pupils, and take a deep personal interest in their welfare, Hindu fathers send their boys, although they know full well that the object the missionary has in teaching is to lead all his students to know and love the Christ. Sometimes this is done with fear and trembling, especially when there have been conversions to Christianity amongst the students. I have heard of parents visiting a Hindu temple and vowing to spend a certain amount in offerings, if the goddess will preserve the faith of the pupil firm to the end of his school or college course.

As a Missionary agency, the importance of this educational work can scarcely be over estimated; for generally the students lose all real faith in the religion of their fathers. This is not to be wondered at, when we remember that the scriptures which the Hindu values so highly speak on almost every subject—philosophy, astronomy, astrology, medicine, mathematics, history, &c.; and as many of them were written thousands of years ago, their teaching does not harmonize with the results of modern scientific researches: *e.g.*, these books teach that the world is a flat plain, triangular in shape; that it rests upon the back of a snake, that the snake stands upon the back of a tortoise: when therefore the tortoise raises one of its feet to obtain a little rest, we get an earthquake. Eclipses of the sun and moon are the result of a giant named Rāhu trying to eat them up. Whenever therefore an eclipse takes place, there is the greatest excitement and hubbub in a Hindu town. The people shriek and yell, beat paraffin oil tins, and use anything that will make a noise to frighten away the giant. Quite on a par with these are other stories told as by the inspiration of the gods. As the Hindu youths study physical geography they see the errors with which their books abound, and naturally their faith in their divine origin is destroyed. But in many cases, although faith in their old books is gone, they continue to worship the images that are set up in their houses, lest they should be put out of caste, and be made to suffer.

In the Mission schools a good English education is given, the boys who have studied in them appearing in the University examinations; but in addition to this about an hour a day is given to the study of the Bible, or books written for the purpose of giving evidences in favour of the Divine origin of Christianity. The matchless example of Christ, in perfect harmony with His verbal teaching, greatly impresses the Hindu. He can find scattered through his own religious books beautiful moral lessons, sometimes most clearly taught; but when he sees that his gods and goddesses are described in those same books as living in direct opposition to the words they taught, these truths cannot exert much influence upon his life. I have frequently heard men say, "As I read the Sermon on the Mount I felt that God is righteous and pure; and further, that all who stand in His presence must also be righteous. To whom could we go for purity? Our deities were worse than ourselves. If they cannot keep themselves pure, how can they make us pure?" There is a common proverb of the people, one I have often heard them use, which conveys a most dreadful condemnation of their religion: "Whilst the teaching of the gods is worthy of being listened to, their example is unworthy of being copied." But they fully admit the superiority of Jesus' life. He taught what was right by His words, and He lived as He taught. The position of most of the educated men towards Jesus Christ is one of profound respect. This results very largely from the example and preaching of one of their greatest modern teachers, who has been dead only a few years, Babu Keshub Chandra Sen.

These Mission Institutions differ largely from each other. Some have classes which teach only to the Entrance or Matriculation standard of the University; others have classes preparing for the B.A. degree. Some have only about eighty or ninety pupils; some have over a thousand. But judged by their results, it seems to me that there can be no doubt that the idea of establishing them was a most wise one, and that at this moment they are an immense power for good. In the Government Institutions the strictest neutrality in religious matters is observed. The Bible is not read in its classes, and no religious instruction is given there. In fact, I have heard of some of the professors who, whilst professedly neutral in religious matters, have really taught infidelity; but this is quite opposed to the spirit of the Government. Those who leave these religiousless schools, however, do not leave them as they entered; their studies as a rule having shattered their faith in the old Hindu system. There is no doubt that immense forces are at work in destroying the old order of religious faith and practice in India.

The aid that these Mission schools render to our work in preaching the gospel is most marked. Young men who for years have read the Bible and other Christian books daily, and come into the closest contact with Christian teachers, know a great deal of Christian truth, and are freed from the prejudices that are so common amongst the people generally. I have often heard these men state in the midst of their old friends in the villages, that all that the missionaries say is true: Christianity is far superior to Hinduism. But only a comparatively small number of them are baptized. The reason of this is, not that they do not believe in Jesus, and love Him too—but when they take this step it compels them to give up home, parents, and all that is dear to them. Were it not for this fact, the number of Christian converts from this work would be very greatly increased.

But although comparatively few of the students in these institutions openly embrace Christianity and unite themselves with the Christian Church, it is from this class that some of the best members of our Native Church have been received. Most of our Bengali ministers and evangelists were either led to become Christians whilst at school, or it was the teaching they received at that time that, quickened by the Holy Spirit, led them in after years, even at the cost of all earthly good, to cast in their lot with the followers of Christ, and, like Moses, to choose rather to suffer affliction with them than to enjoy the pleasures of sin for a season. And I can say this, that it is a most painful experience to witness the struggle going on in the breast of a young man who has won your love, as duty pulls him in one direction, and natural affection for parents in the other. And further, it is a most difficult duty to urge a man to "do the right," when following your counsel is sure to result in the partial, if not complete, separation from home and all old associations. In India to-day, as in most countries when Christianity is first preached, the meaning of Jesus' word, "I came not to send peace but a sword," is realized as it can seldom be in a country nominally Christian.

On Sunday mornings Scripture classes are held, in which a large proportion of the members come from the school. This fact shows very clearly that they are interested in what is taught, and wish to know more of Him who is commended to them as the Teacher and Saviour of men. From personal experience I can say that I know of no work more interesting and pleasurable than that of trying to lead those who have been trained in Hindu homes to understand and accept the truths He came to teach.

CHAPTER XVIII.

WORK AMONGST THE HINDU GIRLS AND WOMEN.

MISSION work amongst the women and girls of India is certainly as interesting and important as any in which the Christian Church is engaged; and as many people in England are showing real interest in it, and are anxious to have a share in it, I shall describe it at some length. It is certain that if the women of England fully realized how greatly their sisters in India need the light and comfort the gospel can give, they would be still more anxious to send them teachers.

To show the necessity for lady missionaries in India, I may say that it is a most exceptional thing for a woman to listen to us as we preach the gospel in the streets of the towns and villages. The wives of the middle and upper classes of Hindu society are kept in seclusion, so that they are never seen by any gentleman excepting those belonging to their own family; whilst the poorer women who may walk to the markets to buy their goods, or to the rivers to bathe, or to the temples with their offerings, consider it improper to stand in a congregation of men, though they are listening to a religious teacher. The village women, again, are so terribly afraid of a European, that when they see one, as a rule they run out of their way rather than come near him. Under these circumstances, in many parts of India the missionary

COURTYARD OF HINDU HOUSE.

has very few opportunities of making the gospel known to them. It is rather mortifying to the pride of those who may glory in their good looks to find that when

Bengali village babies first see their pale faces, they are as frightened at their strange appearance as an English baby would be were a black-skinned negro suddenly to approach them. In travelling in different countries, one finds that each people considers its own type of beauty the highest, just as each crow is said to believe her own little crows the fairest.

The position woman occupies in India is so different from that she holds in England, that it is almost impossible for those who have not seen this at all to realize it. Here she is the equal, there the slave of her husband; and the home life of the people is as opposed to that with which we are familiar as it is possible to conceive.

The Hindu house is built with the object of providing a secluded part for the ladies. There are the public rooms in which the gentlemen spend their days; and there are the Zenāna Khannahs, or women's apartments, quite separate and distinct. The gateway of a respectable Hindu's house leads into a courtyard, such as is represented on the previous page. On the ground floor all round this open yard are the store-rooms and quarters for the servants, &c. On the first floor the sitting-rooms and reception-rooms are situated. But all these rooms are for the gentlemen; no lady member of the house is to be seen in them—at any rate when strangers are present. During the day the gentlemen of the family sit and talk together; but husbands and wives are not supposed even to be seen speaking to each other in the daytime. Here the gentlemen transact their business, receive their friends, and amuse themselves. On the platform opposite to the entrance-gate the images are placed when festivals are held, such as I have described in a previous chapter.

To the right of this platform is a small door, leading by a narrow passage to an inner courtyard, round which are the dining-room, bedrooms, and apartments of the women. At meal times, the gentlemen pass into these inner apartments, where they sit to their food, not with their wives—but to be waited upon by them, as a lady would not think of having a meal until after she had served her husband. In these family mansions there are a great many people living together, as a "family" amongst the Hindus means not husband, wife, and children; but three or four generations of people. In many of these large houses there will be the great-grandfather, his sons, grandsons, and great-grandsons, with their wives and families; and the great-grandfather's brothers and their descendants too. It is rather a tribe or clan than a family that occupies a Hindu house. For when a man marries, he does not have a house of his own; he would not think it wise to leave his wife alone all the day, whilst he was engaged in business. He therefore takes his wife to his father's house, in which a bedroom is given to him; he continuing to live, during the day, with the gentlemen of his family as he did before his marriage: the wife taking her place amongst the ladies. It is more like life in a hotel or barrack than what we associate with the term home. The English meal, where husband, wife, and children sit together at the same table, is unknown amongst the strict Hindus. All the gentlemen of the family take their meals together, seated on mats on the floor, using their right hands without knife or fork or spoon, just as their forefathers did thousands of years ago.

Passing through the doorway that separates the public from the private parts of the house, we come into a smaller courtyard, round which a number of rooms are built. On entering these rooms, we notice a great difference between them and those round the outer courtyard. Whilst the more public rooms are well lighted with large windows, and capitally ventilated, the inner rooms have but very small windows high up in the walls, because the Hindu scriptures teach that a woman must "never stand at a door or look out of a window." So that the women's rooms are, after all, very much like prisons. Generally, a girl will be about eleven or twelve years of age when she leaves her own home and joins her husband; and from the day she comes to her father-in-law's house until her death she is virtually a prisoner. Occasionally after her marriage she may visit her father's house, but to few others would she be permitted to go; and when she goes there she is carried in a palanquin, which is simply a wooden box carried by four men. This conveyance is taken into the inner courtyard; and when the woman enters, the doors are carefully closed, and over this a thick cloth spread, so that as they travel through the streets they can see nothing, nor be seen by any one. Sometimes it is considered necessary for a lady to visit the Ganges to bathe: when she goes there to perform a religious duty she is carried into the water in her palanquin, the doors being closed; and when her bathing is over, she returns in her wet clothes to her home, lest by any chance her face should be seen. In this manner the well-to-do people try to seclude their wives. It is no wonder, therefore, that they should welcome the visits of Christian ladies who sit and talk with them, not only on religious topics, but also tell them some of the wonders of the world which these secluded ladies, alas, are not permitted to visit.

I may perhaps mention here that once I knew of the fetters of custom being broken, and were the opportunity frequent, it might not be easy to rivet them again. In December, 1883, there was a grand Exhibition in Calcutta, where Britain, India, and the Colonies sent some of their most wonderful and beautiful manufactures. Soon this was the talk of the town; and as its wonders were discussed in the Hindu families, the ladies pleaded with their husbands for permission to visit it. The older women were decidedly opposed to so great a violation of custom, and prophesied all kinds of evil if the prisoners were allowed for one day to enjoy liberty. But in tens of thousands of instances the request of the wives was granted. Several days were specially reserved for Hindu ladies; but on ordinary days I saw many wandering through the beautiful courts of the exhibition—some in groups of two or three, some in strings of a dozen, each holding on to the dress of the one in front, and the whole number in charge of some young boy or missionary lady; for although the husbands granted permission to their wives to see the sight, they were not bold enough, save in a few instances, to accompany them. Such was the effect of this violation of Hindu custom that many gentlemen declared that, in their opinion, had the exhibition continued much longer, the ladies, having once been free, would not again have submitted to their imprisonment.

Of course, the great masses of the people do not live in these grand houses. The homes of the people generally are mud huts, each having one centre room and a verandah to the north and south. The verandahs serve as rooms where the family can receive visitors, whilst the room itself is used mostly as a sleeping apartment. As a rule the people have no bedsteads, but sleep on a mat on the floor, with a quilt thrown over them in the cold season. They lie down to rest in the clothes they wear during the day. And in these huts a family, according to our use of the term, live together—*i.e.* husband, wife, and children. As these people have no servants to wait upon them, the wives are free to go to market, &c., as are the women in England; but as I have said above, custom forbids them from standing amongst a crowd of men, though they may be gathered round a Christian preacher.

The position of women is shown to be inferior to that of men from the hour of their birth. As soon as a boy is born, a horn made of a shell is blown to tell the neighbours the good news; but when a daughter is born there is no sound of rejoicing. When a son is born, friends come to congratulate the father; but when he has a little girl, if friends come at all, it is to show their sympathy with the family. For a son, religious ceremonies are performed for the purpose of securing the blessing of Sasthi, the goddess who is believed to be the special guardian of women and children; but for a daughter no such ceremonies are performed. If a man is asked how many children he has, he will tell you the number of his sons, but not mention his daughters. I was greatly surprised the first time I noticed this. Calling upon a gentleman, I asked him what family he had. "I have two children," he said. A little time after, seeing a little girl coming to sit on his knee, whilst the two boys were playing about, I asked who the little girl was. "She is my daughter," he said. "But," I replied, "you said you had only two children; this makes a third." "I said I had two children—there they are; this is only a girl," he said. Mothers with sons are regarded as the favourites of the gods; but mothers with daughters only are thought to be accursed: and the Hindu religion permits a man to marry a second wife if, within seven years of marriage, he has no son, although he may have daughters.

The chief reason of this difference in the treatment of sons and daughters lies in the fact that sons may prove a source of income and profit to the family, and will be able to perform the funeral rites for a father and mother; whilst the daughters must be provided with a husband. This is often a very expensive affair. So difficult, in some castes, is it to obtain a suitable bridegroom, that fathers have had to borrow money, which it has taken them a lifetime to pay off, to meet the expenses of the wedding—as it was necessary for them to give costly jewellery for a wedding present, or they could not induce a father to allow his son to marry their daughter. In some parts of India at this time it is known that many little girls are killed almost as soon as they are born, so that the parents may not have to incur the expense of getting them married. Often little girls of ten or eleven years of age are married to men sixty or seventy years of age; because, whilst their religious customs compel a father to find a husband for them, younger men are not to be found at the price they are able to pay. As widowers may re-marry within a few weeks of a wife's death, and as there are no unmarried women for them to choose from, they are obliged to take some little child whose father had not money enough to spend on the wedding to enable him to find a more suitable husband for her.

Whilst it is lawful for a widower to marry as soon as he wishes after the death of his wife, a widow must not re-marry as long as she lives. It is true that it is now legal for a widow to have a second husband, but fashion, or custom, is against it, and very few are bold enough to defy custom. The lot of Hindu widows, I believe, is as painful as that of any class of women on the face of the earth. In olden times probably thousands of widows were burnt alive every year with the dead bodies of their husbands; but this is now forbidden by the Government. I do not at all wonder, however, that some of these poor women should say, "Why does the Government prevent us from burning with our husbands, when our life is so miserable?" Widows are taught that it is because of some great sin they have committed, either in the present or some former life, that this dreadful calamity has come upon them.

Much as the men of India need the comfort and hope the gospel offers, if possible the women need this still more. As girls of five years of age, the religious duties that are allowed them are to make offerings to the gods that they will provide them with a husband; that this husband may have a long life; and that all sorts of dreadful things may happen to her if their husband takes a second wife. When they are married, they are allowed to make a gift or offer a prayer to the gods only in the name of their husband. And when they have a son, their own name is lost; they are called, not Tulsi, or Kāmini, as the case may be, but Priya's mother, or Durga Dass' mother. It is therefore not surprising that when they have read to them the fourth chapter of St. John, which gives the account of Jesus' conversation with the woman of Samaria, the women ask in astonishment, "Is this true? Did Jesus, whom you say is the great Saviour, talk to, and give religious instruction to, a woman?" It is "good news" indeed to them to learn that God loves His daughters as He loves His sons; that He is ever ready to hear their prayers, and to give them the blessings they require.

The mothers of India will exert a mighty influence for good over their sons when, instead of being prejudiced against the gospel, they themselves know and love Jesus. The most absurd and dreadful stories are told by the Hindus of what Christianity is. Quite recently I read of a Hindu calmly declaring that the missionary keeps a pot of old beef and pork, and that when a man comes for baptism a scavenger is called to bring some of this meat for the convert to eat before he is baptized. It would be impossible for a Hindu to imagine anything more dreadful than this. Meat, and especially beef, is hateful to him. Yet this is the kind of stories that circulate in Hindu society. And the women, being profoundly superstitious and excessively religious, have proved the greatest hinderers of our mission work. But as they are taught in our schools and in their homes by Christian ladies, and learn what the Christian religion is, we shall have them as our truest helpers. When this day dawns, the conversion of India to Christ will not be far distant.

Now I must give some account of the way in which ladies carry on their work in India. Great Britain, America, and our Australian colonies, are all sending their representatives to take part in this intensely interesting and all-important work.

First there are schools for Hindu girls. These are now flourishing; but it was not always so. For years the prejudice against female education was so strong, that only the poor and low-caste people would allow their daughters to be taught, and these had to be paid to come to school. Until about forty years ago it was almost impossible to find a woman who was able to read, and I question if there was one indigenous girls' school in all India. The older women were very strongly opposed to any change in their customs in this matter, and declared that the gods would severely punish any who learned to read. And when some of the little girls who had been taught lost their husbands, it was declared that this was a direct punishment for opposing the customs of the country.

But this prejudice has now largely passed away, at any rate in the cities. As education has spread amongst the boys, the desire for educated wives has led to a very great change in the treatment of girls. When Dr. Duff was urging missionaries to educate the boys, he said, "Let this educational work go on for thirty years, and female education must follow." And his words were true. Now-a-days, a girl who is educated is far more easily married than one who is ignorant. Parents, therefore, who might otherwise not wish to send their daughters to school, are very glad to do so, or to provide some one to teach them at home.

The schools are situated generally in a quiet lane or street in the middle of a Hindu village or suburb. Sometimes schools are built for the purpose; sometimes rooms are rented in Hindu houses. The girls attend from the time they are about six, until they are eleven or twelve years of age. As they have a distance to walk, and there is always a danger of their being robbed of the jewels they wear, in addition to teachers, Hurkārus, as they are called, *i.e.* women servants, have to be engaged to bring the children to and take them from school. It is a pretty sight to see one of these old women with a string of ten or a a dozen bright-faced little girls, with their books and slates under their arms, toddling off to school, that they may learn to read, write, and sew, and thus be provided with some means of instruction and amusement when they are old enough to become prisoners in their husband's homes.

At present we have not a sufficient supply of educated women to teach in all the girls' schools. Generally a Bengali Christian woman has charge, and Hindu Pundits are engaged to teach most of the subjects. These institutions are under the care and watchful supervision of European ladies, who have been sent out from Christian lands to engage in this work, or have been engaged in India. And, as I know from experience, it is a most interesting work to teach these little girls, who, but for the Mission schools, would be left in utter ignorance.

Many of these school-girls are married. They have a little spot of red paint on the forehead, at the parting of the hair, and an iron wire bracelet on the wrist—the sign of marriage in India. As a rule they are married when about seven or eight years of age, but continue to remain at home until they are about eleven or twelve. Occasionally they go on a visit to their father-in-law's house before the time comes for them to go there for good, that they may know him and his friends. This is the courting time in India; but it is after the marriage bond is formed; no dislike or incongruity of disposition can loosen it. These visits, sometimes prolonged, materially interfere with the school work.

In these schools an ordinary education is given in Bengali. The Gospels, and such books as "Line upon Line," are read in the classes; so that when the pupils leave they know almost as much of the historical parts of the Bible as girls of the same age in England. They learn to use the needle too. This is never taught in the Hindu home. There is no dressmaking, as the Sāri, the dress of the women, comes from Manchester just as it is woven, ready for wear. And if the men wear clothes that need cutting and sewing, this work is done by tailors. The ordinary Hindu women can neither read nor sew; when they remain uneducated, their life in the Zenāna Khannahs is necessarily most monotonous. But the power to read, and to use the needle, which they gain in our schools, in addition to the religious instruction they receive, is an incalculable blessing to them when they grow up to womanhood.

Some of these little girls are widows. Volumes might be written and yet fail to exhaust all the sad meaning of that simple statement. When the marriage knot is tied, though bridegroom and bride are but children, and have never lived together, if the boy die the girl is a widow, and has to suffer all the woes of widowhood. On my last visit to one of these schools I saw a little girl of nine summers, whose husband had died a few weeks previously. At so tender an age she could not realize her position; but after a few years the sadness and sorrow of her life would commence, without a ray of hope to brighten it. The aim of the legislators of India was to make the lot of the widow as painful as possible, that they might ever be thinking of the husband they had lost, and be ready to join him in the next life; and certainly these law-givers have succeeded in arranging a life of misery for them.

The school-girl's life ends when she is about eleven or twelve years of age, as she then has to leave her home and become an inmate of her husband's family. From this date she can appear at school no more, but must commence her life of seclusion. It was when some of these children were leaving school that they put what seemed to be a very simple question to their teacher, Mrs. Mullens, but it proved to be a question leading to the most important results. They said, "As we cannot come to school any longer, *cannot you visit us?*" Up to this time occasionally a Christian lady had entered the recesses of the Hindu house, but no systematic work had been done there,

Mrs. Mullens and her daughters commenced a work which has developed far beyond their most sanguine expectations, and which will go on until the home-life of India is completely changed.

This work bears the name of Zenāna work. I have heard of most strange meanings given to this really simple, though to English ears strange-sounding, word. I have heard the opinion expressed that Zenāna was a country in Africa! And that it is a province of India! But it is nothing of the kind. Zenāna simply means "a woman." Many of the Mussulmāns of India speak of their wives as their Zenānas: the women's apartments of the house glory in the name of Zenāna Khannahs. Zenāna work simply means mission work as it is carried on amongst the women in their homes. It was commenced in a very simple and natural manner: it has grown within a very few years into what I believe to be the most important that man or woman can undertake for the good of the millions of India.

In many cases arrangements are made by which a Bengali teacher visits a house two or three times a week, the European lady paying a weekly visit to superintend her teacher, and also to impart religious instruction. From the commencement of this work it was made a condition of a lady undertaking to teach Hindu ladies, that she should be perfectly free to give Christian teaching. At first a little opposition was raised; but no serious difficulty has arisen since. It is an immense blessing that a lady confers upon the inmates of these homes when she gives simply a secular education; but it is a still greater good when she can lead the women to know and love the Saviour. Thousands of ladies, young and old, are now being taught in Bengal, who, but for this Zenāna agency, would have remained in the grossest ignorance.

There is no doubt that in the hot and rainy seasons it is a trying work, as it necessitates travelling in the hottest parts of the day, and sitting for hours in hot and badly ventilated rooms. For a few weeks during the hot season, the visits are paid in the early morning; but during the greater part of the year, when the gentlemen of the family are away at their business, the Zenāna teacher finds the ladies of the household free to receive her. But trying though it be, it is a most interesting work. Nearly all those engaged in it are charmed with it, as one would expect them to be.

Many stories might be told to show the good that results from it. One day I was travelling at a distance from Calcutta, when a Hindu gentleman came up to me and said, "I have a great deal to thank the missionaries for. I am now living here, whilst my wife is at my family house in Calcutta; but I can write to her and receive a letter regularly from her. And this I owe to your Missionary Society." A large number of the educated gentlemen are separated from their families for months, often years together. Those in Government service are drafted to different places, and with very few exceptions they go alone, leaving their wife and children in the care of their family at home. When a wife is uneducated, there is no direct communication between her and her husband for months or even years together. Occasionally a letter might be sent to the family, which the wife would share with others; but if she could neither read nor write there could be no real correspondence between them. Educated men complain bitterly of the fact that between themselves and their uneducated wives there can be but little in common. True fellowship there cannot be. It is impossible for English people who have not come into personal contact with the educated and ignorant of India, fully to realize what a vast change education makes; what new worlds it opens to men's view. Often for weeks together I have been living in boat or tent with uneducated Bengalis. After the first half-hour conversation begins to flag. There are comparatively few subjects in common between us. But with educated Bengali gentlemen I have spent many a pleasant month. I can therefore quite understand the loneliness of which an educated Hindu complains when married to an uneducated woman.

There is no doubt whatever that in Bengali homes there are many ladies whose love to Jesus is real and intense, and who there are trying to serve Him. Some have been baptized; but very few compared with the many who are truly Christian in heart and life. The ladies engaged in this work, rightly I think, do not urge the Hindu ladies to be baptized; because were they to receive this rite, they would have to leave their husband, family and home; and, from their past secluded life, are quite unfitted to earn their own living. The time is coming when this difficulty of baptism will be overcome, and then the multitudes of secret disciples will boldly declare their faith. The confession of faith in Christianity may be made by word without any serious persecution: it is baptism alone that cuts a person off from the Hindu community.

I scarcely know of any greater change in the spirit of a people, than that which has come over the Bengalis within a generation respecting female education. About forty years ago, the homes of the people were closed against the Christian visitor: now in the neighbourhood of Calcutta there are more houses open to receive the visits of Christian ladies than there are visitors to go. In some of the houses now it is not at all uncommon for evangelistic services to be held—reading, singing, prayer, preaching by the missionary ladies, European and Bengali; and as a result of this, the foolish prejudices and the gross ignorance of the people respecting Christianity are quickly passing away. Were there more earnest Christian women to undertake this work, and were there more self-sacrifice on the part of those who cannot themselves go, but who can send others, the darkness that for so long has settled in the land, would quickly pass away, and the slavery which has for so long enthralled the women would give place to freedom.

INDIAN WATER JARS.

CHAPTER XIX.

INDIA'S NEED.

FROM what has been said in previous chapters, it will be evident that India's need of the gospel is great; in this chapter a few facts will be stated, gathering as in a focus the spiritual necessities of the Hindus, in the hope that those who possess this knowledge, having "freely received, will freely give" it them.

1. India needs to be taught that the God of heaven loves His children with a Father's love.

As the truth concerning the infinite love of God has been familiar to English Christians from their infancy, they imagine that of course everybody must know that God loves man, and that He is ever ready to give them every good gift that they desire. But a little familiarity with the religious books of India, and with the ordinary beliefs of the people, soon removes this error. The books speak of the lives the gods live in heaven, and also of their many appearances on earth; but excepting those that have been written since Christianity was preached in South India, some few centuries ago, none of them speak of this feature of God's character. The people are found in great numbers visiting the temples with their gifts; it is not, however, love that draws, but fear that drives them there. It is because they are taught that the gods are either indifferent to them and must have their interest excited, or are hostile and must have their anger appeased in this manner, that they bring their gifts to their altars. In the olden time, before the British rule was established in the country, it was known that the judges were open to receive bribes, to lead them to decide a case in favour of the giver, and that he who gave the most costly gift would win his case in court. In a similar spirit the people go to the temples to-day, thinking that they can bribe the gods to do their bidding. They give a small gift in the hope of getting a bigger one in return.

This is the natural result of the teaching which is common in their books, that the gods exist upon the gifts of the people. That, somehow, a goat sacrificed to Kāli, or fruit given to Siva, or water from a holy river poured upon a stone to represent Vishnu, reaches these deities and satisfies their hunger and thirst.

Again and again one of the gods is said to have come down to the earth in order to lead men into sin, because as long as they were good and prosperous they gave but trifling gifts. A god leading men to sin, that when its punishment came upon them, they might give largely to obtain deliverance! This is the teaching of the Hindu scriptures.

The evil of this teaching respecting the gods is seen again in the fact that there is constant rivalry between them; the devout worship of one being a cause of jealousy to another. One god, pleased with the devotion of a man, confers some blessing upon him; another discovers a way by which this blessing may be turned into a curse, or, though fulfilled in the letter, violated in spirit. As in times of civil war the people of a country are made to suffer by both the contending parties, their sympathies for the one side being a reason for the attacks of the other; so India is constantly in this position with her many gods, who not only fight amongst themselves, but wreak their vengeance on the worshippers of their rivals.

In the ordinary life of the people, belief in the existence and power of many deities is a constant source of misery, as they cannot tell whom they may happen unintentionally to offend. Every evil that comes to a man is believed to be a direct punishment inflicted by some god. A child is sick, and as the father watches its pain and weakness, his heart is sad. Gladly would he take the place of his child, or do anything he could to save it. He first goes to his family god with a gift, in the hope that his prayer will be heard. Seeing no change, he goes to a neighbouring temple with a similar object. Again disappointed, he goes to a second, third, and so on, until his money is all spent, or the child passes away, leaving the father's heart nearly broken. What consolation has that poor parent? He is certain that some god is angry with him, but which of the many he cannot find out. He believes that it is because of some neglect of duty that this punishment has come: it may be in his present life; it may be in some life he lived thousands of years before. He is sure of this, however, that could he only have found out what he had done wrong, or whom he had offended, he could have made it all right with a gift, and so have saved his child from suffering and death.

Another illustration of this evil may be seen in the fact that every Hindu must worship, and thus try to keep on good terms with, all the gods that are known. If it is believed that one god has given a son, as soon as it is born a goddess must be induced by a gift to take care of it in its childhood. A third must be chosen as its own peculiar object of worship; and as the days for the worship of any deity comes round, a gift must be presented to them. Some Brāhmans get over the difficulty in a strange manner. After worshipping their own god, and making an offering of fruits and flowers, &c., to it, they throw a handful of rice upon the ground without mentioning any names, and let the whole company of gods scramble for it; each taking what he considers his share.

Now any one who thinks at all on this subject must feel that India needs to be taught that there is but *One* God; and that He is wise—mighty—loving—good: more ready to give us good gifts than an earthly father is to give good things to his children. It is a comfort in the hour of sickness, pain, sorrow, bereavement, to feel that "One above, in perfect wisdom, perfect love, is working for the best;" to know that "all things work together for good, to them that love God." To be certain that we are in the hands of One who cannot err, and who is ever ready to bless without our doing anything to make Him love us. But this truth is wanting in the sacred books of India.

2. India needs to know that God loves *all* His children, and that however they differ in character and position, they are brethren because children of One great Father.

How different from this the common belief of the Hindus! They are taught that at first God divided man into four great classes; that the Brāhmans, being the most highly favoured, sprang from His head, the warriors from His arms, the merchants from His thighs, and the servants from His feet. Although we have classes in English society—aristocrats and commoners; rich and poor; learned and ignorant; pure and lapsed—yet we know that these distinctions are made by man, not by God; and further, that it is possible for the lowest to rise from the depths and attain to the highest position in the land. But the Hindu is taught that as a man is born, he must continue; that during his present life it is impossible for him to become different from what he is. He is in the class in which God has placed him, and from this he cannot by any possibility rise.

Taught by his religious books, the Hindu again divides man into two classes—Hindus, and non-Hindus; and no word in English is so expressive of contempt as is the word "Mlechha," by which we, as well as all other people who are not Hindus, are known. And although they believe that we, as long as we are Christians, cannot possibly enter the heaven of the Hindus, they have no "way of salvation" to offer to us. Heaven is for the Hindus; there is no room there for others, nor any way to it except by being born in a Hindu family. Sometimes gentlemen have rather amused me as they have suggested that possibly, as a reward for leaving England and living in India in order to benefit the people, the gods might reward me in my next earthly life by arranging for me to come on earth as a son of a Hindu. I can honestly say I have no wish to receive this mark of distinction; but can now more than ever

> ". . . thank the goodness and the grace
> That on my birth have smiled,
> And made me in this Christian land
> A happy English child."

Amongst those who are born Hindus, the class distinctions are far greater than anything that exists amongst ourselves. It is no uncommon thing to see well-dressed men prostrate themselves before an almost naked Brāhman; and I have seen low-caste men take the dust from a Brāhman's foot and put it on his head, and even drink the water in which a Brāhman has washed his feet. This is the result of the immense influence these men are believed to exert over the gods; in some cases they are actually worshipped as divine beings. Between the members of the same caste there is a good deal of brotherly feeling; but for those of a lower caste there is the greatest contempt felt and shown. A man of a low caste would be allowed to die of hunger or thirst, before many of those of a superior one would give him food or drink.

But, if possible, the contempt for all outside of the Hindu system is even more marked still. In the Rāmāyana, one of the most popular of Hindu books, which is largely filled with the life of the god Rāma, we read of an immense army of monkeys which greatly assisted the god in regaining possession of his wife Sita, who was stolen from him. These monkeys are described as clever, brave, faithful friends. Who were they? The people who lived in India before the Hindus came there; and as they were not included in any of the castes, and followed the teaching of a religion different from Hinduism, they are called monkeys in a book that is said to have been inspired of God. And to this day, although the Hindus are very kind and hospitable, many of them would almost as readily touch a toad as an Englishman. But as a strange punishment for this contempt, the Hindus have come to worship Sugriva, the king of the monkeys, and Hanumān, his commander-in-chief.

There is, however, this consolation for us, that we as well as the Hindus are parts of God, and at one time were amongst the favoured classes; but though now through sins in former lives degraded, in due time we may hope to come into the world as Hindus, and then have another chance of climbing up to the heaven of the gods. At least, this is what their books teach: we are English, and not

Hindus, because of our past sins; when we have endured all the punishment these sins deserve, it will be possible for us again to be Hindus and then obtain the privileges they enjoy.

From all this it is clear to those who reflect, that India's need of the gospel is great, since it teaches us that "God is no respecter of persons"; and that the greatest bliss on earth that His service can give, and the highest rewards in heaven, are within reach of all His children. That His love is as great to the poor and the despised amongst men, as it is to those who are reckoned as noble and great.

3. India needs to know the way unto the Father.

It is most surprising, in reading the Hindu scriptures and talking with the people, to find how many ways there are by which a man may obtain "mukti," salvation; and at the same time how contradictory their teaching on this most important question really is. For not only do the books teach that these many ways will lead to God, but they say often that these are each *the* way, by which all must go. The mind gets bewildered with the variety of methods and the contradictions that abound. Some hold that there is no such thing as sin. That as each man is part of God, he can only think, speak, and act as God impels. These men, quite in harmony with the words of their scriptures, declare that the distinctness between right and wrong, purity and impurity, truth and falsehood, have no real existence, but are merely an ignorant way of looking at conduct. Some, again, say that forgiveness cannot possibly be obtained for any sin. By a decree that the gods even cannot set aside, every action has its own reward or punishment, and consequently all who do these things, must necessarily enjoy the reward or suffer the penalty affixed. Others again believe, and act upon the belief, that to bathe in the Ganges will take away all their sins, past, present, and future.

When, therefore, men think seriously of the future, and realize that soon they must appear in the presence of the Judge of all, they are at a loss to know what to do. They read their books and get answers that flatly contradict each other: they go to their priests and receive equally unsatisfactory replies. Men have told me that for years they have gone from teacher to teacher, vainly asking for the true way of peace; but alas, though they have tried them all, they confess that they are farther away from it than when they commenced their search. They tried to please all, but really pleased none; and have lost their time and money into the bargain. How striking an illustration does India present of the words of the prophet, "My people have committed two evils; they have forsaken me the fountain of living waters, and have hewed out for themselves cisterns, broken cisterns, that can hold no water." The thirst of the soul after God is there, and though other gods have been formed to take His place, the thirst remains unquenched until it finds its true and proper supply. Familiar as we are with the truth, the statement comes with marvellous freshness and beauty to the honest but deluded searchers after God in India, "God so loved the world that He gave His only begotten Son, that whosoever believeth in Him shall not perish, but obtain everlasting life." And, again, the assurance of salvation that we have as we receive

Him—for "he that believeth on the Son *hath* everlasting life"—is felt to be a most blessed gift.

4. India needs to know the truth respecting the future life that has been given to us by Jesus.

If the question, "If a man die, will he live again?" be put to a Hindu, without the slightest hesitation he will reply, "Live again? Yes, of course he will; we each have lived hundreds or thousands of lives, and shall yet live hundreds or thousands of lives. This is only one short link in an immensely long chain." But if you ask him what he was, and did, in any of his past lives, of course he cannot tell you; and if you ask whether the memories of the present life will go with him, he will confess he cannot say. The common idea is this. Every living being is a part of, and came out from, God, just as the web is drawn out from the spider's body. And as the tortoise puts forth its legs and then draws them back as it wishes, so God, having for His own amusement caused living beings to exist, when He wishes, He will cause all to return to Him. It may be hundreds of thousands of years ere this circle of lives is complete, but at last all must return to Him from whom they came forth; and then, just a drop of water falling into the ocean ceases to exist as a separate drop, so each human soul will lose its separate existence, and live on for ever as a part of God.

Anything more injurious in its influence upon life it would be difficult to imagine. If a man believes that his actions are not his own, but that he as part of God is forced to act in a certain manner, he simply does what he wishes at the moment. And certainly the people who hold this opinion, are the worst, morally, that one has met with. If a man believes himself free to do as he likes, unfortunately he likes to do what he ought not, and does not like to do what he ought. It is when a man feels that there is a law to guide, and a Righteous Judge to sentence, that he asks, What is my duty? and is impelled to try to do it.

Again, when a man cannot say in any part of his existence whether he is being rewarded for good or punished for evil, what inducement is there for him to turn from evil to good? "Good and evil" do indeed "happen alike to all." If a life's actions are entirely forgotten at death, how can any impulse to do well come from any previous existence?

But it is the hopelessness, the despair that this teaching produces, that makes its evil more apparent. "We bring no memories of the past with us; we carry none with us into the next life," says the Hindu; then, all the ties of relationship and friendship are snapped at death. No wonder that the wail of the mother is so sad and heartrending as she sees the lifeless form of her darling child carried away to be burned. Mother and son loved, but now are parted for ever. No wonder that friends should "weep as those who have no hope," when death snatches away those who were dearer than life. To its followers in such hours of supreme grief, Hinduism has no word of comfort. The most that it can say is "that death is common to the race." To such the words of the Saviour, "I am the Resurrection and the Life," "Thy friend shall rise again," are as cold water to the parched soil, and the shadow of a rock in a weary land. No wonder that Hindu mothers are astonished and comforted as they hear that the child of their affection is not lost, but that again they shall clasp him to their bosom; and that the Hindu widow's heart is made glad with the assurance that death is to her but the portal to a higher life, when she will be re-united to her beloved husband. The wail of bereaved wives and mothers in India even now seems to ring in my ears. The future world to India is "as a land of darkness and the shadow of death."

5. India needs to know what is the reasonable service God requires of man.

The cry, "What does the Lord thy God require?" is certainly one that India asks; and from her teachers one that she asks in vain. When a man says, "What must I do to be saved?" a Guru says, "Repeat your text regularly, and give heed to my instructions, and you will be saved. For I am all-powerful with the gods, and can secure your welfare." After a time, as he goes on with this, a man meets with him, and tells him that if he wishes to be safe after death he must go on a pilgrimage to some distant temple, or to some particularly holy place on the banks of the Ganges. To enable him to undertake this journey he has to find a considerable sum of money for travelling expenses, and also for gifts to the temples he must visit. After this he is told that the way to secure heaven and the good-will of the gods is to build a temple or dig a tank. So he sets himself to work out his salvation by this means. Next he is informed that he must die on the banks of the Ganges, or all his good works will be lost. So he leaves his home and hires a house in the sacred city of Benares. But yet again he hears that unless his funeral rites are properly performed he cannot enter heaven; and so his mind is distracted with the thought that this may be neglected. All through life he is called upon to perform a long list of duties, none of which can have any purifying, ennobling effect upon his character; and as he looks into himself, he cannot see that they have brought him any nearer in spirit to the Supreme God who is said to be holy, pure, and good.

Or again, if we look into the temples themselves to see what is going on there, we cannot see that in the most sacred places the worship is at all able to restoro man to God's image. The service consists in presenting flowers and fruits, in bowings and prostrations, in the repeating of texts in an unknown tongue, and in dressing, adorning, and feeding a lifeless image, as though it were a living man or woman. When, therefore, the question arises, What does God require? there is no answer such as Hosea gave, "To do justly, to love mercy, and to walk humbly with thy God;" or again, "Pure religion and undefiled before God and the Father is this: to visit the fatherless and the widow in their affliction, and to keep oneself unspotted from the world." No wonder that it is absolutely true, that a man may at the same time be a most devout and religious Hindu, and a most impure and untruthful man.

What, then, does India need? The pure example Jesus has given as a revelation of God's will; an assurance of God's infinite love; a mighty motive to lead from a life of selfishness and sin to one of purity and love; the knowledge of God's readiness to forgive. In a word, the truth about God the Father and Friend of man; Jesus the Saviour and Teacher; the Spirit as the Quickener and Purifier of man's spiritual nature. With these truths faithfully proclaimed, there is no doubt whatever that the Light of the world will chase away India's darkness as He has done and is doing that of other lands; and the very religiousness of India, rightly directed, will make her one of the most glorious empires of the loving Saviour and King.

But how can these blessings be given to her? By living men and women, who, at Jesus' call, lovingly and patiently proclaim these truths in schools, in houses, and in the streets, and who have faith to work and patience to wait for the promised blessing on faithful labour. It is not enough to remain with folded arms and pray "Thy kingdom come." Not thus was Britain's power and authority set up in so many parts of the world; nor will it be by such methods that God's kingdom will come and His will be done. The history of the past centuries of the Church show this most clearly:—that where good work was done, the prayer of faith was heard; but that where there was simply the uplifting of the voice in prayer, the blessing, though asked, was withheld.